London Crossings

Literature, Culture and Identity

Series Editor: Bruce King

This series is concerned with the ways in which literature and cultures are influenced by the complexities and complications of identity. It looks at the ways in which identities are explored, mapped, defined and challenged in the arts where boundaries are often overlapping, contested and re-mapped. It considers how differences, conflicts and change are felt and expressed. It investigates how such categories as race, class, gender, sexuality, ethnicity, nation, exile, diaspora and multiculturalism have come about. It discusses how these categories co-exist and their relationship to the individual, particular situations, the artist and the arts.

Published titles:

1492: The Poetics of Diaspora
    John Docker
Imagining Insiders: Africa and the Question of Belonging
    Mineke Schipper
The Intimate Empire: Reading Women's Autobiography
    Gillian Whitlock
Yesterday, Tomorrow: Voices from the Somali Diaspora
    Nuruddin Farah

London Crossings

A Biography of Black Britain

MIKE PHILLIPS

CONTINUUM
London and New York

Continuum
The Tower Building, 11 York Road, London SE1 7NX
370 Lexington Avenue, New York NY 10017-6503

First published 2001

British Library Cataloguing-in-Publication Data
A catalogue record for this book is available from the British Library.

ISBN 0–8264–5292–2 (hardback)

Versions of the stories 'Have a Nice Day', 'The Smell of the Coast', 'Jean and Dinah', 'Que Linda' and 'Such a Nice Kid' were first published in *Smell of the Coast* by Mike Phillips (Akira Press, 1987).

Quotations in Chapter 2 about the Gordon Riots are taken from *King Mob* by Christopher Hibbert (Longman, 1958) and from *The London Hanged* by Peter Linebaugh (Penguin, 1991).

Typeset by Kenneth Burnley, Wirral, Cheshire
Printed and bound in Great Britain

Contents

For Kwesi and Kip

The same time will come

Introduction

I arrived in London on the third day of January 1956. It was a dark, gloomy day. I don't know now what I had been expecting, but what I experienced was a combination of familiarity and strangeness. The city was familiar because I had encountered it so frequently in books, films and travellers' tales. It was strange because the London I knew was a city which existed only in my imagination, a place assembled in my mind out of stories about the past, hints and half-digested fables. Nowadays, when I try to remember the event, there's a peculiar balance about the fact that my memories of life before London have the same fragmentary and sporadic quality. Looking back on those times, it's as if I'm viewing a huge dark canvas where tiny areas of light appear at random, illuminating unpredictable and surprising details.

What I remember in any one moment is a jumble of impressions, like viewing a confetti of scattered snapshots. I was born within the sound of the sea, and the background music to every day of my childhood was the beat of the surf pounding the shore, a perfect rhythm which rocked me to sleep and which, waking up, was the only sound I could hear. Walking to school, I watched vultures circling high in the bright glare of the sky. Sometimes I stared into the sun, squeezing my eyes almost shut to catch the precise shape of the bluish-white disc. Then there was the whirring noise of the parrots' wings as they ascended in unison, flying out of the mango trees where they roosted. During the day our parrots were green, yellow and red, but when I got up to watch them in the half-light before dawn, they were grey shapes, swooping and climbing towards the fading stars. In the same moment the cocks would begin to crow, answering each other up and down the street and across the back-yards. We lived in a narrow road paved with white marl and sand. There were perfect little seashells pressed into the surface. In the middle of this track were parallel ruts made by the wheels of loaded donkey carts. In the grass verges I hunted for grasshoppers, and when darkness fell a chorus of frogs emerged from the canals which ran along both sides. Behind our house there was another canal, more like a small and tranquil river, dammed at one end by a high bank of earth covered with long grass, where all the children in the neighbouring streets played. Grassdam, we called it. On the other side of this river, the milkman, Sadhu, stabled his cows. You could smell them all night, cowshit mingling with something warm and animal, the sweet breath of cows. At dawn he milked them, his head pushed into their sides. Then he washed himself in the river and prayed. In front of him were a few small brass pots full of milk and a heap of red hibiscus flowers. At the end he poured the milk into the bells of the flowers, one by one, and gently placed them in the water, where they floated slowly away, the crimson petals beaded with drops of milk. It was this same canal into which my younger brother, little Mac, toddled and drowned, caught floating among the water lilies. They buried him in a little white coffin. Before the funeral I stood next to the coffin, gazing at him. He was covered in white lilies of the valley, which gave off a strong, dizzying scent. Black ants crawled in a line up the side of the box, and I stood there obsessively picking them off and crushing them between my fingers, until my mother came and led me away.

After that we moved to the other side of the road, away from the river. In the rainy season, after a couple of wet days, rain pounding on the roof like the blows of a hammer, the canals overflowed, and, in the morning, our new house stood in a lake stained brown and yellow by the mud. All the houses rested on columns of wood or concrete blocks, so the water never came high enough to flood them, but these were the most exciting times. In the yard there were several fruit trees – mangoes, star apples, guavas, pomegranates, limes. If I climbed to the top of the tallest tree, I could stand swaying on a branch and see the market clock in the distance, standing out erect over the tops of the houses. The roofs were mostly zinc, and some were brand-new, a sparkling silver which threw back a blaze of sunshine. At the other end of the scale the oldest aged into a deep warm brown. Between these extremes a palette of colours shifted and changed as the sun moved through the sky. At noon the roofs burned bright and furious, churning the air above them into a shimmering haze. At sundown they glowed sweetly as they caught the last red streaks of light. Inside the house at night, lizards climbed over the walls and the ceiling, changing colour as they went, from spots on grey to the purest white. Sometimes they fell to the floor from somewhere above, with a soft, barely audible, plop.

At school we played ring games, boys and girls standing in a circle holding hands and singing, while two or three stood in the middle to act out the narrative. 'Old Rogers' was my favourite. *'Old Rogers was dead and he lay in the ground, lay in the ground, lay in the ground,'* we sang. This was the first line of the story in which an old lady came to pick Old Rogers's favourite mangoes, and the dead man was so infuriated that he got out of the grave and chased her away. One morning in the schoolyard I raced Atkinson over our usual course, once around the concrete blocks on which the school stood. We were both about five years old, evenly matched, and sprinting two abreast around the second corner I banged my knee into the edge of the concrete post. It opened a deep gash, and a teacher took me to the hospital, where a nurse sewed me up while he flirted with my teacher. I don't remember her, but I can never forget the man's face. He grinned a lot, showing a gold tooth in the front of his mouth, and sometimes he took two or three jabs to get the needle into my flesh. I screamed, and when I screamed his grin grew wider. My father was still in the army then, and when he came home from the barracks a few days later, he took one look at my swollen knee and began rumbling angrily. Next day he took me to the soldiers' clinic, where two white men tutted over my knee, sprinkled powder on it, and gave me an injection. After that I got better.

Later on I went to another school. My route there went past the Muslim orphanage where my best friend Ali lived. He used to wait for me every morning outside the gates, a neat white cap cocked on his head, the khaki uniform the orphans wore pressed into perfect creases. We sat in pairs at desks with a double seat, and Ali always sat next to me. This was an Anglican school, and every morning we sang hymns and said prayers. The ritual was Christian, and I don't know what Ali thought of that, but he had a way of changing the words in the hymns and the prayers which made me giggle like crazy. 'The Father, Son and Holy Goat,' he'd say solemnly, and look sideways at me, which made me crack up. One morning Mr Dyer crept up behind us and laid two stripes across my back with his bamboo cane. That didn't stop us, but afterwards we were always looking out for old Dyer and the swish of his cane. On the way home from school one day, we stood in a circle of people watching two men fight. They were wrestling on the ground, and suddenly one of them screamed, a frightening sound. 'Leggo me seeds,' he shouted over and over. A crazed-looking woman thrust herself through the circle and threw herself on the men. 'Leggo the seeds. Leggo the seeds,' she shouted in her turn, the three of them writhing and tumbling over each other. Everyone in the crowd laughed. Someone took up the chant, and Ali and I joined in: 'Leggo the seeds.' When I got home I asked my mother what these seeds were, but she just laughed.

One night I was wandering alone in the village, drawn like a moth to the lights of the cinema. Standing outside gazing at the photographs, I was suddenly surrounded by some big boys who began pushing me from one to the other, laughing at my tears. Without warning, inexplicably, my mother appeared and gave one of them an almighty shove. 'Leave him alone.' The big boys stepped back, still laughing. After that I stayed home at night. By day we hunted rats through the backyards, a gang of screeching small boys led by half a dozen hysterical dogs. Mostly we didn't catch them, and when darkness fell the rats became the hunters. Everyone in the street kept a little flock of chickens or ducks, and at sundown we shooed them into the wire-netting runs or cages where they slept, the cocks stalking in majestically as if they didn't give a damn. When there were newborn chicks in the run the rats gathered, tunnelling and gnawing at the wire mesh all night long. On one of these nights we heard a commotion and came down into the yard to find that two rats had got into one of the cages where there was a hen with three baby chicks. The chicks' bodies, yellow fluff matted with red, were strewn about the cage. One rat was already dead, its head pecked into a bloody mess by the hen, who was now crouched in one corner staring, as if hypnotized, at the other rat, which was running about the box in a frenzy, jumping and throwing itself at the mesh, desperately trying to escape through the hole by which it had entered. Even from a distance of yards we could smell the rats' sewer stink. Uncle Aubrey was already there. He had blocked the hole and, moving with his habitual deliberation, fetched a can of kerosene and began pouring it into the cage. The rat seemed to know what was coming, and once it felt the splash of the kerosene it went mad, its body springing and convulsing, dealing out a series of heavy blows against the walls of the cage. Uncle Aubrey lit a match and dropped it in, and the scene exploded in flames. The stink of burning rat and chicken feathers combined was sickening, and although my mother pushed me back up the stairs before I could see the rat die, the smell haunted me for days.

Death seemed never to be far away. As he was running through the yards one day, a rusty nail stuck in my cousin Lennie's foot. It happened practically every week, and didn't seem to matter, but in a couple of days Lennie began to droop, and in an incredibly short time he developed lockjaw and died. The sweet smell of the lilies haunted the funeral, and standing by his grave I wondered why him and not me. All the backyards were littered with rusty pieces of metal and nails. I was wounded in the same manner many times both before and after that event, but that particular rusty nail was waiting only for him.

Every week a procession of Indians wound its way through the street, past the house. These weren't the big gatherings, like weddings; merely family and friends celebrating something domestic, such as a baby's first haircut. A black man named Joe Taylor usually led them, beating a goatskin drum. From time to time he squatted down by the grass verge, dug a hole and lit a small fire over which he warmed up his drums, while some of the women danced and sang, their saris swinging, and others moved around distributing sweets and cakes among the crowd of people who poured out of the houses to greet them. After a while Joe would start up again, the sound of his drum sharp and ringing – a-rak-a-tak-a-tang-a-rak-a-tang-a-tang-tang. But this was ordinary, everyday stuff. When Vikram, the boy who lived next door, got married, it was different. Arriving at the house in a carriage drawn by a pair of large mules, he stepped out into the mob of spectators dressed in a robe which shone with gold and silver, a tall, shining crown on his head. His hand moved and he showered a handful of coins into the crowd. I had known him all my life, but now he was a glittering stranger. Seeing me staring, he winked. Vikram's father, Driver, lived in a hammock under their house. They called him Driver because he was once the foreman of a gang on the sugar estates, but now he was a sick man – or that was how he looked. All night you could hear him, coughing and hawking and spitting into a tin pail he kept beside his hammock. Sometimes he screamed or shouted in his sleep. He always said the same thing: 'Go away. Go away. I didn't kill you.' I stayed awake to hear it one night, then I was so frightened that the next few nights I stuffed my ears with cotton wool. 'It's his conscience,' my big brother said. The funny thing was that I really liked Driver. Every time he saw me he pulled a face and smiled. I loved his wife too, a motherly woman who let us sit in their house and watch her cooking. It was like a show sometimes. Cooking roti she plucked a round of dough off the fire, threw it in the air and clapped it twice between her hands, all in one smooth movement.

In the only photograph I possess of myself at the age of 4 or 5, I'm sitting facing the camera, my face empty of experience or desire, nothing but a slightly puzzled and eager curiosity in my expression. I don't remember posing for the photograph, or anything about the occasion. I'm not even certain whether this is a photo of me or my cousin Lennie. Nowadays I remember only the sharp, overpowering smell of raw sugar, and the feel of its thick grains in my fingers. All this was before I came to London, and as I write about this time it's as if I am summoning up ancient messages from a static, unchanging universe, isolated outside the currents of time. I'm also aware that the period I'm recalling was a moment of dramatic transformation. A ferment of political and cultural change was simmering around me, but my own memories, innocent of such knowledge, are to do with sights and sounds and smells. For instance, when I think of the politics of the time, I remember torches flickering in the night and the press of crowds around me at election time, or I remember soldiers with pink faces, their kilts and berets signalling an incongruous gaiety, their guns carefully outstretched, like awkward metal babies.

At this distance, reading the history of that period, I understand what I was seeing. So the act of remembering is now an effort of reconstruction, my impressions assembled out of fragments whose meaning is relevant only to my present self, rather than a record of my past. In these memories I am hardly there, an observer rather than an actor, and it's impossible to trace a firm outline of what and who I was, or to describe an identity to which I could put a name or which existed before my life changed.

In my mind, the moment of leaving Guyana is like an impenetrable wall beyond which only these fragments survive, if only because the process was remarkably similar to the way I imagine death. If I had been older I might have had a choice: to go or not to go. As a child I knew only that I would leave my home on a certain date. I knew I was unlikely to return in the near future, if ever. I dreaded the prospect of the departure. I was apprehensive about being alone during the long sea voyage, and I was almost completely ignorant about the place to which I was going. My only certainty was that my mother and father would be waiting on the other side. I had no relationships, apart from my immediate family, which could survive my absence. Later on in my life I might have written letters, telephoned, or in some way clutched at the bonds of a mutual past; but my childhood friendships had been ephemeral. In the years following my departure, the older people I had known died, the younger ones scattered, leaving as I had left, to disappear into some distant landscape. Of the classmates I had in that time, I only ever encountered two or three in later life, and only one of those could remember who I was. On my departure, I had become a ghost. I left hardly a trace behind me, and I took nothing with me apart from a series of fading tableaux.

One picture continues to haunt me. On the morning that I left we travelled to the docks in Mr Nightingale's creaking taxi. As the car reached the end of our street I looked up to see a long line of boys and girls, all of whom I had known for the whole of my life, standing by the side of the road. Seeing me, they began shouting and waving, but I don't remember waving back. Instead, I burst into tears.

Even now, when I recollect this event, tears well up in my eyes, and each time I ask myself why. Am I crying in pity for the grief I felt as a child? Am I crying for my long-lost home? Is it some sentimental reflex? Is the memory real, and if it is, what does it mean?

— 1 —

Born Again –
London, 1956 to 1960

When I woke up on my first morning in London, I heard the familiar sound of the waves crashing and retreating. For a moment I didn't know where I was; then I remembered I was in London, and I began wondering how long it would take to get to the beach. After a while, though, I realized that this pounding rhythm was the sound of traffic. It was a moment of sheer grief and horror. This was my first impression of London, and it took a long time before I became accustomed to the fact that nothing in it was like anything I had ever known.

In that sense, arriving in England was like being born again. During the long sea voyage I'd had almost a month to get used to the idea, but coming down the gangplank I had no list of expectations, no sense of entitlement to a specific career, no landmarks which would tell me where to go or what to do. Apart from the fact that I would be with my parents again I had no idea what would happen to me. My future was a clean slate. At the same time, over the next few months, I used to find myself following the outlines of the life I would have been leading if I hadn't come to England. It was as if I'd had a limb amputated, leaving a constant flow of sensations through the nerves, which repeatedly summoned up non-existent feelings and events – the highlights of my past experience, Christmas, New Year's Eve, school sports day. I kept asking myself, if I'd still been there, what would I have been doing? Recalling my state of mind, it was as if I was trying to blot out my surroundings, to crawl my way back into the comfort of my former life. I didn't do it with any great energy, however. Somehow, I already knew that I was never going back. In less than a year my life before England had already receded into the realm of fantasy, something that my imagination played with as a refuge from the reality around me.

On the other hand, now that I had been transported to such an impossible distance from my familiar self, the overwhelming problem I faced was the need to answer the question of who I was, and my first instinct was to try and master my new environment.

On the morning of 4 January 1956, shortly after being awoken by the noise of traffic, I began inventing London. I use the word *inventing* because the London I inhabit still seems to me a city brought to life by my experience, memory and imagination. There are stretches of it into which I have never ventured, and which I am unlikely to visit except by accident. At the other end of the scale, there are parts of it – buildings, open spaces and entire streets -which no longer exist, but which have a presence in my mental map of the place. So this London of mine is partly an abstraction which I have assembled in defiance of time and geography. Over the time in which I lived in the city I needed to do this again and again, because the city meant a great deal more to me than just the site where I progressed from childhood to adulthood.

We lived in Islington during those first years, on the top floor of a three-storey house in Southgate Road. There were three other families living on the lower floors, and a clothing factory in the basement. The area wasn't desperately poor, like neighbouring Dalston in Hackney, but the street was lined with similar houses, nearly all of them occupied by several families, bursting with people. As it happened, I had arrived just in time to be part of a life which was about to disappear. During that first week I became familiar with the landmarks which, for a while, were to outline the limits of my existence. Oddly enough, these features remain in my mind as signposts to the new world I entered, but, in reality, they were already fading into the past.

For instance, a couple of hundred yards away from the house, in Ball's Pond Road, there was a blacksmith's forge, a dark cavern ringing with the sound of metal on metal, where the coalmen and the rag-and-bone men took their horses to be shoed. A few minutes' walk away was the building which housed the public baths near Dalston, a dingy palace lined with glazed brick and tiles. Along the streets trolleybuses lumbered, lit by sudden showers of sparks like tiny fireflies, the singing wires signalling their approach. From the chimneys plumes of dark smoke billowed towards the grey haze of the sky. Faced with this landscape it was easy to read the city as a sort of historical map, a record of lives which stretched back into a distant past. I got the same impression from the layout of the house in which we lived. It had been built at some point during the nineteenth century, and it had obviously been intended to house only one family. A short flight of stone steps led down to the basement, now walled in and separate from the rest of the house. Another flight of steps led, between two columns, to a porch, beyond which was a massive door. Inside, the rooms on the lower floors seemed huge, with long windows stretching almost to the height of the ceilings, picture rails, elaborate ceiling roses, marble mantelpieces and fireplaces with cast-iron grates. The rooms at the top were about half their size, and easier to keep warm in winter. The landing at the head of the stairs was our kitchen – a stove, a sink and a gas water-heater squeezed into a space just large enough for one person to move around. The furniture in the rooms was old and dark: beds with intricately carved headboards, spindly chairs and tables, and big solid wardrobes with brass fittings. Much later on I often saw the same kind of furniture for sale, refurbished and gleaming in stores and antique shops; but, at the time, everything around us seemed worn, used and indelibly marked by other presences. It was as if we were camping in a house which had been abandoned, and sometimes, at the back of my mind, I had the feeling that one day the rightful owner would reappear and demand the return of his property.

This sense of our presence being temporary and provisional was, as far as I can remember, shared by all the migrants we knew. By tradition, men from our region looked for work and advancement abroad. My uncles had worked, on and off, in the Trinidad oilfields, in Panama, in Costa Rica and in Florida. My father had travelled the eastern Caribbean looking for a foothold, before trying England. On leaving school my older sister, my brother and their classmates had scattered, some to the University of the West Indies in Jamaica, some to Brazil and Venezuela, others to colleges in the USA or Britain. For anyone with almost any ambition, spending a period of time in another country was inevitable.

We also knew that when we got to wherever we were going, the kind of work we did or the conditions in which we lived were almost an irrelevance. Our goal was the future, and at the moment of arrival no one felt themselves to be defined by their workplace or their neighbourhood. The stigmata of class and status had not yet become ours, and our citizenship was not yet in doubt. Our role was simply to occupy whatever spaces we could find. Work was good, shelter was necessary, and the time and place constituted a kind of limbo within which we prepared ourselves for whatever might come next.

To my parents and their friends, London was merely different – colder than Caracas, and not as strange as New York. They talked continually about the city, offering each other bits of information about how it worked, outlining conditions in the places where they lived and describing the odd customs they encountered. But they had no sense that this was a radical clash with an alien culture, or that they were experiencing a species of shock. They had always known about the sights and sounds of the city, and in any case, they didn't regard the way they had been brought up and lived as a 'culture'. In a new place it was expedient and appropriate to adopt different manners, and to learn different skills. It was as simple as that. When we thought about what was happening to us it was in terms of an encounter with the variety of customs which made up the city – a world of industrial processes, of speed, of change and of endless mobility. For this meeting we were curiously suitable – already rootless, alienated and supremely adaptable.

My mother worked in a workshop which made fur coats. Her employers were a Jewish couple who had arrived in London as refugees from Germany. The only other employee apart from my mother was an Irishwoman called Peggy. The workshop was in Petherton Road, a street which ran between Islington and Stoke Newington, ending up a couple of hundred yards away from the house where Daniel Defoe once lived. I used to fantasize that Defoe would have been enthralled by the conversations which went on between my mother and her three friends as they sat in the tiny room, the women endlessly pedalling at their sewing machines, while the man, short and fat with round gold spectacles, worked the steam press, disappearing every few minutes in a cloud of vapour. They were indefatigably curious about each other, and my mother came home each evening with some new morsel of information about male behaviour in Donegal, or Jewish wedding customs in pre-war Europe.

'You wouldn't think,' my mother whispered, as she brought me to the workshop for the first time, 'to look at them, that those people have been through so much.'

The world in which they had lived fascinated her. Sometimes she screeched with laughter when she talked about her friend Peggy, who had frequent rows with her husband, which always seemed to terminate with his abject apologies as he served her tea in bed. 'Tea in bed,' my mother would repeat derisively. 'Tea in bed.' No one could imagine my father behaving in such a servile fashion, but there was something wistful about the way my mother related these stories. At other times her voice throbbed with emotion when she talked about how her employers had fled across Europe in fear of their lives. Describing the hardships they had endured, or their tales of massacres and disappearances, her eyes grew moist. When she talked like this I always felt puzzled about the fact that she could summon up so much sympathy for the troubles of these strangers. Later on I guessed that, in their difficult lives, she could see a reflection of her own experience, and shedding a tear for them gave her the comforting feeling that she was not alone.

In comparison, I was deeply troubled by my initial encounters with the people of the world I had entered. At school the work was easy enough. I had been placed in a class which seemed to be repeating the work I had done over the previous two years in my old school, so I had no trouble staying ahead of my classmates. It was some time before I realized I had been stuck in the lowest academic stream with a prize selection of the craziest, most disruptive pupils, and the problems I faced didn't have much to do with race or racial differences. Instead they were largely about the style and content of working-class life in London.

In the mornings, before a teacher entered the room, a clutch of boys would be squirming in one corner, bollock-grabbing, a species of wrestling in which the goal was to squeeze each other's testicles. A typical day would begin with up to a dozen boys jammed into a shouting, swearing heap, newcomers hurdling the desks and throwing themselves into the fray. The rest huddled around the radiators or sprawled on top of the desks, discussing the events of the previous night. During breaks the bollock-grabbers retreated to the bicycle sheds by the side of the playground to entertain themselves by spitting on the ceiling, leaving long stalactites of saliva to drip slowly onto the bikes and heads of other boys. No one protested, partly because the champion of the spitters, Ernie, although still a junior, was easily the largest boy in the school. Almost grotesquely bulky for his age, Ernie had other notable talents. For instance, he could stand at the far end of the urinals and hit the entrance with a well-aimed jet. As it happened, Ernie's ostentatious spitting and pissing were deceptive. Due to his formidable appearance he never became involved in any of the fights which occurred practically every day, and, in comparison with most of our classmates, his manners were gentle and polite. But if one of my schoolmates back in Guyana had behaved in this way, I would have assumed he was insane. Here in London Ernie's manners seemed normal, as did the lunatic aggression of the other boys. By lunchtime on my first day I had heard the word 'fuck' more often than I ever had in my entire life, but by this time I was beginning to understand the etiquette of the classroom. My first, characteristic mistake had been to stand up and greet the teacher when he came into the room, as I had been trained to do at my former school. Everyone laughed and jeered, while the teacher gave me a puzzled stare and told me to sit down. In a few seconds I had learned that the way to avoid trouble was to keep my mouth shut and be unobtrusive. After the first day I avoided speaking until I could reproduce the language of the school. A large minority of boys in the class had the same problem. I had gravitated, by some process which seemed involuntary, to the corner of the room where the 'foreign' boys sat. We were all recent arrivals, one Turk and three Greeks from Cyprus, a Jamaican, a Burmese, a mixed-race boy from Liverpool, a Welsh boy and an Asian from Kenya, who decamped to a private school in the suburbs after one term. Most of these were bilingual, but we all spoke English with varying degrees of fluency.

English was my native language, but it probably would have been simpler if I had learned the language from scratch. For example, I came from a country where the use of English was an important and highly valued instrument. The dialect we spoke at home and in the streets was riddled with newly invented metaphors and images. In the playground one of our games was to make up insulting rhymes about each other, and the most versatile talkers would stand toe-to-toe spinning out verses until the weakest flinched. Extraordinary witticisms and turns of speech from political rallies or lawcourts were repeated with relish, and public figures who were skilled at manipulating rhetorical tricks were frequently quoted with respect and affection. In comparison, the language I heard from my teachers in London seemed brutally direct and tediously clichéd. In much the same way my classmates' language was painfully obscene, their insults devoid of art or imagination. I was familiar with words like fuck, piss, shit, cunt, bastard and bloody; but I had never spoken them aloud in routine conversation. Nor had I heard them used in such a casual and vacuous manner. What I found even more inhibiting was the curt, brusque tone of the language at school, or in the streets and the shops. In the normal run of things, most of the whites whom I encountered sounded as if they were trying to be intentionally rude most of the time.

I couldn't grasp it at the time, but I think now that I was hearing the sound of the city, a public language which reflected the mechanized patterns of day-to-day urban life, chopped down meaning into tidy blocks which could only serve specific functions, and which stripped words of ambiguity and emotion. In this idiom all kinds of contradictory meanings – tenderness and anger, uncertainty and rage, hatred and love – could be fused together and expelled in a single blunt expletive: fuck.

At night I practised imitating the accents I heard, carefully rehearsing the glottal stop and the nasal shortening of words, but, even then, it was obvious to me that there was something more to mastering this dialect. The way the boys at school spoke was an expression of how they felt, and how their minds worked. When I tried to speak in the same way I could hear a false note, like a mocking parody, and for a few months I avoided speaking to anyone outside my family unless they addressed me directly.

I had found myself in an upside-down world from which there was no escape, and during the first few months it would have been impossible to imagine knowing or liking the city. It seemed too immense to know, and too dangerous to like. As I remember it now, my world was a dreary landscape of grimy stone through which I moved, fast and furtive, between areas of safety – school, home, the public library or the cinemas. Speed and caution had become essential skills. The riots at Notting Hill were still a couple of years ahead, but we lived on the border of one of the most violent and disorderly districts in London, and every day brought news of black men being beaten up by young thugs, or stabbed in a brawl.

I didn't begin breaking out of the familiar circuit that had become my prison until the end of the school year. This was 1956. I was going to be thirteen years old and it was my first summer in London. As the vacation approached I realized that once the school gates closed I wouldn't know what to do with myself, because I didn't yet know anyone outside the limits of the school playground. On the other hand, not having to face the classroom bullies for a couple of months was a blessed relief. So the onset of the holidays found me torn between trepidation and delight.

In retrospect the sun seemed to be shining all the time, but there was no question of going away on holiday. For my father the season was a heaven-sent opportunity for overtime, and he took the view that his white fellow workers were completely mad to spend the year accumulating savings, only to blow it all in a couple of weeks. The rest of the family worked all day too, and after the first week pacing around and gazing out of the window I knew I had to do something, so I set out to learn about London. That wasn't as simple as it sounds.

The city, everyone warned me, was dangerous and unpredictable, especially for me.

For a while I confined myself to wandering around my own district. I would start the day by going to the nearest swimming pool, then wandering into Clissold Park, which had a pen containing deer and rabbits. Sometimes a snatch of music, or a name, brings the precise flavour of that time back to me – the strange look of the sky, with the sun gleaming out from behind the banks of grey and white clouds, the trees covered with the bumpy fruit they said were called conkers and which you couldn't eat. After a few days the deer got to know me well enough not to run off when I talked to them, and they were the only creatures I had a conversation with during those weeks. My only friends I called them, because this was a time when I'd have happily left my parents and walked back home if there hadn't been an ocean in between.

But I was young, curiosity and boredom conquering misery, and in a few days I began travelling by bus to the West End, then walking back by various different routes. During the first week I went to the public library and drew up a list of monuments and buildings to look at – the Tate Gallery, the British Museum, the Embankment, Trafalgar Square. What I remember was the odd sense of everything being unexplored and mysterious, but at the same time somehow already part of my memory. Walking on Waterloo Bridge for the first time I recognized the view immediately. I had read about all this, in textbooks, in novels, especially Dickens's novels, and although it wasn't very much like the way they described it, everything seemed half-familiar, like something emerging from my imagination.

The loneliness, terror and isolation of that summer is unforgettable, but so is the feeling of liberation, the sense that I was being born again into a new self. I've never again had a summer in which my emotions were so chaotic and intense. It was the beginning of the time when the city reshaped me and made me part of what it was becoming.

London was already a violent place. Apart from the routine spate of fist fights or stabbings which took place every weekend after the pubs closed, the newspapers carried a fearsome litany of gang murders in Soho, Hackney and the East End. At the time, the atmosphere of violence which surrounded us seemed like an inevitable, more or less natural part of city life. In London, war was more than a memory; for instance, although the wartime bombs were more than a decade in the past, the occasional street on my way to school was still disfigured by piles of rubble. In the decade since the end of the Second World War, Britain's conscript army had been fighting insurgents in various parts of the world: Korea, Malaya, East Africa and Cyprus. A large proportion of the boys in my classroom had relatives who had been killed or injured or were still soldiering in one conflict or the other. Some had brothers in the armed forces and were looking forward to joining up themselves. Successive waves of demobilization had fed back into the population generations of young men whose rite of passage had been the rituals of war. During the same period the devastation in Europe, followed by a series of colonial upheavals, had brought refugees and migrant workers from all over the globe. In the middle of the city a festering clutch of slums in East and West London were the site of constant struggles for living space between English people who had lived in the same slums for generations and the rafts of displaced newcomers. In this arena of competing claims, families like mine were the latest, most vulnerable enemy.

This was the world in which I began shaping myself to grow up. At the same time it was having unpredictable effects on me. I joined the school's boxing team during my first year. Part of my motive for doing this was my envy of another boy, Philip Dathorne. Philip had been living in London for a couple of years, but our familes were closely intertwined. They had been neighbours back home and we had played together when we were babies. Our older brothers had been classmates, and Philip's uncle had married my aunt. In my first week, our parents put us together as if it was a foregone conclusion that he would be my mentor. The problem was that Philip had already crossed the barricades I was now facing, and he moved in the currents of the city like a fish in water. His speech was the speech of a Londoner, larded with strange words – bint, spunk, shag – and he seemed to have no fear of the streets. Listening to his stories about clubs and dancing and places which were only names to me, I felt inadequate and depressed. In comparison I felt myself to be miserable and restricted, a prisoner of my own fears.

There was no logic to my becoming a boxer, because I had never boxed or been interested in the sport, but training with the toughest kids in the school seemed a way of breaking out of my isolation. In the gym I did what I was told, banging away at the punchbag and doing endless press-ups, and within a couple of weeks I had been entered for a match against another school. I didn't know enough to be scared, and I didn't have the expertise to shuffle around sparring like the boxers in previous bouts, but I was determined not to look foolish. This time, I thought, I would find out what it was like to take a beating, and I'd also find out whether I could fight back. When I climbed into the ring and found myself confronted by another boy, I followed my instinct and hit him. Afterwards I could not remember what happened next. All sensation seemed to disappear, until the referee pulled me away and shoved me into one of the corners. Opposite me the other boy was crouched against the ropes, blood dripping from his nose and staining his vest. For the first time I noticed that the gym was packed, and the noise of the kids' screaming rocketed round the walls, a deafening din, and it took a few moments before I realized I had won. The experience, however, was oddly disturbing, because the half-minute in which I had apparently been ferociously pummelling my opponent was a period I couldn't recall, a complete blackout; and even while my team mates were patting me on the back and congratulating me, I knew that something strange and dangerous had happened.

I never agreed to fight in another match, but I had gained a reputation as a tough nut which lasted for the rest of my time at the school, and the bullies stopped treading on my toes or spitting on my blazer. On the other hand I now had an image to maintain, and when someone offered to sell me a flick-knife with a six-inch blade I gave him a week's dinner money without a qualm.

Over the next couple of years my relationship to life in the city changed dramatically. I became part of a tightly knit bunch of 'foreigners'. A few English boys were part of our group, but, at school, most of the others gave us a wide berth, perhaps because we always seemed to be in some kind of trouble. In the circumstances this was no surprise. The year of my migration was also the year that rock 'n' roll arrived in the city, bringing with it tight trousers, long hair and a new style of gang warfare. The wave of movies about juvenile delinquency spilling out of Hollywood provided a style manual. Some of them, like *Blackboard Jungle*, were popular in spite of their stern moral messages. Others fed a kind of hysteria which was the flip side of a nascent youth culture. For example, the cinema was crowded with teenage boys when they showed *Six Boys and a Gun*, a story in which six boys set out to rob a store and accidentally kill someone. While under arrest, they spend the night arguing about who committed the act, with the police and their parents trying to persuade each one in turn to testify against the others. The drama becomes a clash of conflicting loyalties, full of lines which we quoted repeatedly in the playground over the following weeks. One line I still remember came when one of the gang turned on the killer – 'There's only room for one in that chair, Eddie, and I ain't sitting on your lap.' The climax comes at dawn when it appears that the boys will be forced to identify the shooter. Instead, each one attempts to exonerate his comrades by confessing to the murder.

In London, the audience for *Six Boys and a Gun* belonged to a generation of working-class youths, cut off from the disciplined hierarchies of their elders and re-creating social life in a fragmented city. The message was both powerful and ambiguous. In the district where I lived every café, cinema or club seemed to be the territory of a group of boys who demonstrated their ownership and solidarity by picking a fight with unwary strangers. At the time teenage West Indians were actually few and far between, because migration was still a mere trickle in comparison with the flood of the early 1960s. Walking in the streets, or at any gathering of young people, the colour of my skin was an unmistakable signal, like a flashing beacon; and any of the boys who befriended me at these times was taking a considerable risk.

See me now in the winter of 1957, walking down Blackstock Road towards Finsbury Park. I am with Theo, Papa, Geoff, Kenny and

Bobby. We walk in a solid group because it looks more intimidating. Other kids leave you alone unless they're in a larger group. We are dressed in the fashion preferred by boys – fourteen- to sixteen-year-olds – in North London. Two-button drape jackets. Trousers sewn tight to our legs. Shoes with thick soles – *brothel-creepers* and *winkle-pickers.* Theo and Papa are Greek, Geoff is Jamaican. Kenny is a dark Burmese with a hot temper, whose hair falls over his forehead in a curl, just like Elvis. He is the only one of us who possesses a leather jacket, and, like Bobby, he's a champion boxer, well known in the district. We are going to the Hollywood, a dance-hall near the park. It is a sort of crossroads between various territories, and teenagers from all over this part of the city encounter each other here. The girls come to dance and be seen, showing off their tight sweaters or backless and sleeveless dresses under their cardies. The boys pretend not to look, lamp each other and pick fights. The Hollywood is actually a central point in a compass. About a mile to the south, between us and Camden Town, is the Nag's Head, ruled by the legendary Flanagan brothers and their Irish henchmen. North-west is Muswell Hill. To the east is the Blue Kettle caff, focus of the mobs from the Angel and Hoxton.

There are elements in the crowd from all these places, and it makes for an explosive mixture in which I'm as nervous as a cat because we are all immigrants, apart from Bobby. Theo and Papa might be able to blend into the crowd at a pinch, but Geoff and I are, as usual, the only West Indians in sight. We are a little younger than the sixteen- and seventeen-year-old kids who come here, but that simply makes us more vulnerable, and we know that if trouble starts we'll be an immediate target. In normal times there are ways of avoiding confrontations. Stay away from the bad Teds, don't meet their eyes, don't go to the gents if you can help it. At the same time I just know that we'll be lucky to get out without a fight. Once inside, we meet Maureen and her friends from the neighbouring school. She's second-generation Irish, pretty, with black hair, melting dark eyes and a slender, mobile body. Everybody watches while she's dancing, and the Irish boys glare at anyone else who gets too close to her. The fact that she's mad about Kenny is a major source of annoyance to them. In the slow dances Maureen presses herself against him, her arms around his neck and her head resting on his shoulder, and before long there are little knots of Teds standing about, staring and following Kenny around between dances. Half-way through the evening, it happens. Turner, a big Ted from near the Caledonian Road, whose dislike of wogs is notorious and who fancies Maureen into the bargain, bumps into Kenny and pushes him away angrily. 'Are you screwing me, mate?' he asks, which is the conventional signal in these parts for starting a confrontation. Kenny, no hesitation, hits him in the face. Turner's friends pile in immediately and surround Kenny. We pile in to rescue our friend. The place erupts, girls screaming and boys running towards the action. Everyone seems to be hitting us. I hit back, but most of my efforts are devoted to getting out, although I'm keeping my eyes open for knives. Eventually we're out, and I'm running past the park gates with the rest of the boys. They've stopped chasing us and we go towards Kenny's house in one of the streets opposite the park. Outside we stand around waiting for him. Theo and Papa are bleeding, and I'm not sure what we're doing, but I don't want to go off on my own. Suddenly Kenny reappears. 'Come on,' he says. We look at each other, and then Kenny opens his jacket and shows us the hatchet tucked into his belt. He turns and walks back down the road, moving fast. Theo is the first to react. Ten years later he'll be a doctor, and even now he's the most stable and sensible of our group. 'Grab him,' he shouts, and together we surround Kenny, talking to him, telling him to calm down, it's not worth it, the police will be around, anything we can think of.

After the night of the hatchet I made a determined effort to avoid situations of this kind. I had the insistent feeling that sooner or later one of us would be killed or seriously injured, and in my memory of that time the city remains an arena crawling with macho confrontations over one kind of territory or the other. At the same time I couldn't get rid of the uneasy feeling that whatever happened to me was willed, a conscious act. Perhaps it had started in the moment when I lost myself in the boxing ring, but it was as if I had surrendered and begun to embrace everything I had first hated about my environment. At the start of my journey I had dreamed of floating towards wide horizons. Instead, I felt like a rat scurrying through a dark tunnel.

My frustration was compounded by the mystery of my brother's disappearance. Four or five years earlier my brother Ivor had left for London with my parents, and since then I had heard nothing from him. He was about six years my senior, and I had last seen him standing at the side of a boat as it chugged away from the docks. He was, in the way of big brothers, my hero, more intelligent, more capable than I could imagine. When I arrived in London I kept on asking where he was and when he would come to see us. My parents' replies were evasive, and the story emerged in scattered bits of anguished reminiscence. The real answer was that they had no idea what had happened to my brother or where he was.

A year after they arrived in England they had woken up to find him gone. He had simply never returned home, and they never heard from him again. He was only seventeen years old, and in our experience it was an unimaginable event. Families and friends quarrelled and separated, but a complete disappearance was different, and after a while my parents were convinced he was dead. My sisters and I learned not to talk about the subject, but the mystery of my brother lay like a dark secret at the heart of every event. In the way of such things, everyone who had known him thought that someone else must know more than they did. Everyone who knew the story blamed my father's nagging, but even if that were true it couldn't explain why my brother had cut himself off from everyone and everything he knew. Sometimes my mother's sorrow was like a cloud which cast a shadow over us all, and when at odd moments we found her weeping, there was no need to ask why.

From time to time I set out to trace Ivor's footsteps, but there were no clues, no trail I could follow. The nearest I came at the time was an encounter with his best friend, Philip Dathorne's older brother Ronald, who was then a postgraduate student at Sheffield. My father had spoken his name with a grim anger. He had questioned Ronald, he said, who claimed to know nothing, but it was while under Ronald's influence that my brother had taken to bad habits. They smoked dope, he told me, and wore berets, walking around looking like pimps and pretending to be artists or poets or some such thing. Suitably primed, I pumped Philip about his brother's movements and eventually tracked Ronald down to the public library in Islington during one of his visits to London. He told me what he'd told my father. He had seen my brother a few days before his disappearance, but he hadn't a clue where Ivor had gone or why. After this I gave up, and more or less resigned myself to the idea that my brother's absence was permanent. Even so the mystery nagged at me. Something had happened to him, I knew, which was to do with the currents of life in the city, and perhaps the same thing was happening to me. The idea terrified and, at the same time, fascinated me. It was possible, I thought now, to simply let go and lose myself.

Oddly enough, my encounter with my brother's friend Ronald had introduced me to a radically different strain of ideas. He lived in a wide, strange world. He talked about Civil Rights in the USA, about African independence and about poetry. He studied with a famous poet, William Empson, and he had met and talked with some of the authors whose names were blazoned on the bookshelves around us – Selvon, Lamming, Naipaul. Men like ourselves, from the same place and the same experience, who were creating literature about what it meant to be people like us. He was writing a novel himself, he said, about the experience of coming to London and the people whom he had met. My brother, he hinted, and his strange fate, would be a central theme in his book. All this in a couple of conversations before he went back to Sheffield, but it was as if a bright light had illuminated my world and I could have listened to him forever. I had been thinking of myself as peculiar, perhaps a little mad, but now I could imagine my emotions as being linked with something outside myself. My encounter with Dathorne was like a counterweight to the longing I had felt for my missing brother, and in the next year my direction had changed again. I began haunting the library, and hanging around with some students I met there, and who knew Dathorne. One or two had been friends of my brother, and for that reason, I suspect, tolerated the constant presence of an eager and naive sixteen-year-old schoolboy.

As it happened, it was fortunate that I had stopped frequenting the usual teenage haunts, because this was 1958, the year of the Notting Hill riots, and the momentary conjuncture of teenage gang violence and fascist polemics against immigrants had made the streets more dangerous than ever before. Our part of North London was some distance from the area of West London where the riots were taking place, but we had lived near Ridley Road market, a stronghold of Oswald Mosley's blackshirt politics, and we were accustomed to hearing ourselves denounced and abused in the streets or the media. The stories and pictures in which mobs besieged black people's houses or beat up black men on the streets were no surprise. During the week of the riots, whenever we went out, the air seemed to pulsate around us as if in expectation of some happening. On the other hand, although the thought of mob violence was terrifying in the abstract, we had lived with it for too long to do more than tread with caution. At night I acquired the lifelong habit of walking on the extreme edge of the pavement or in the street in case someone was hiding behind the hedge, and my ears were preternaturally tuned to the most distant sounds. No one, I knew, would catch me by surprise. If I had to die, as some of the older men said, I would take someone with me.

Another element had entered our lives with the riots. On my way home one night, as I prepared to get off the bus, the conductress, a middle-aged woman with a kind face, smiled at me. 'Be quick now,' she said. 'Run home safe.' 'If I ever get home,' I snarled back at her. 'We're not all like that,' she said, crestfallen. It was an insignificant exchange, but it was the first time I had entered into any kind of dialogue with a white person about the anger which seemed to surround us. We had taken it for granted that the coldness and hostility of the English was integral to their nature, like their attachment to pubs or tea-breaks; and what made it more settled and somehow more cruel was their pretence of neutrality. I knew, for instance, that on many occasions the colour of my skin was like a red rag to a bull, but everyone – my classmates, the teachers, the newspapers – seemed anxious to deny the truth of the matter. After the Notting Hill riots, however, no one could prevaricate about my experience. At school, for instance, the fights I got into around the district had earned me a reputation as a hooligan. Now, in the playground and the classroom, everyone began taking sides. The louts argued that it was all the fault of the immigrants, who shouldn't be here anyway. 'Going down Notting Hill tonight,' they would announce, just within earshot, 'for a bit of a giggle.' Other boys, usually those in the upper academic stream about to go into the sixth form, frowned importantly and commented that it was no laughing matter. The 'foreigners' closed ranks. During the breaks, we occupied a corner of the playground and played ostentatiously with our knives. Oddly enough we felt a new kind of distinction, because, it seemed, from being a sordid segment of the urban landscape, unmentionable in polite society, we had moved to being the central focus of the nation's attention.

After school, I spent most of my time with Boston, a law student who had been one of my brother's classmates. Like most of his friends he lived a life of bohemian precariousness, doing whatever jobs he could find to support himself. He shared a room in a rambling house near Highbury Fields. It had once been a hotel, but now it was owned by a Jamaican who had turned it into a kind of flea-pit, stuffed with young transients, two or three at a time, stacked in the tiny rooms. On the ground floor there was a club consisting of a bar and a jukebox, which played American R&B, alongside the Jamaican imitations which were the precursor of ska. It was the only place in the district where young black men could be confident of being admitted, and at the weekends the club was crowded. The police raided it every week, it seemed, looking for drugs or runaways among the white girls who came there, or responding to neighbours' complaints about noise and fighting. It was obviously only a matter of time before they closed the club down, but in the months after the riots an atmosphere of hysterical recklessness seemed to grip us, and the parties grew wilder and more crowded. By this time I had lost my fear of the streets. Paradoxically, the riots had given me a feeling of greater security. The worst had happened, but it was no more than I already knew. This was the moment when the worst crisis occurred.

I was walking home from the club at about ten in the evening. Boston had walked half-way with me up to Highbury Corner, where he was due to turn back. I forget now what we were talking about, but we stood at the junction opposite Highbury Station near one of the stalls which sold tea, sandwiches and ugly sausages called saveloys. In those days there used to be one of these stalls at every major junction, always surrounded by a small crowd of people, and it was a measure of our indifference to danger that we paid no attention to the men standing nearby. In the middle of one of Boston's jokes, however, something caught my attention. Somehow, without grasping its import, I'd been hearing the word *nigger* for the last couple of minutes, and when I looked over towards the nearest knot of men, I realized they had begun to drift closer and were now only a few feet away, glaring ferociously at us. There were three of them. The man in the centre, and apparently the leader, was the smallest. He was buttoned up in a dirty raincoat. Above the scarf around his neck was a snarling mouth, a Hitler moustache and bulging eyes. Behind him loomed two larger men in donkey jackets, but I hardly noticed them because, the moment I laid eyes on the little man, I wanted to laugh at his ludicrous appearance. In the next moment I had begun to burn with rage. 'What you looking at, black boy?' he said, moving a little closer. 'Do you want a slap in the face?' Automatically I put my hand in my pocket, took out the knife and flicked it open. The little man appeared not to notice and he kept on coming towards me, his mouth opening and closing. I never knew what he was saying because my senses, hearing, sight and smell seemed to focus on what was about to happen. The knife was a comforting weight in my hand, and all I could think of was the spot just above the third button of the raincoat where I was going to stick him. Time slowed to a crawl, and in my memory the little man's mouth, a black hole below his twitching moustache, is wide open, his face a plastic mask arranging itself into odd postures like a series of comic stills. I was holding the knife down by my side, and Boston told me later that he heard the click of the blade. Immediately, he grabbed my arm and twisted me away, throwing me half-way across the road, then pushed me towards the park behind us. Half-walking, half-running back across Highbury Fields, hearing the men shouting behind us, I seemed to be waking from a moment of unconsciousness, with the same roaring surprise I had felt after my boxing match. 'You shouldn't carry that thing around,' Boston said reprovingly. 'You could have killed that guy.'

Hearing this, I couldn't stop myself laughing, because if only he'd known it, killing the man was exactly what I had intended, and only his quick thinking had stopped me.

Since that time, more than forty years ago, my view of what was happening to me has gone through a series of changes. Reading accounts about the migrants and our experiences in that time, I'm struck by the extent to which they restrict themselves to arguments about race and racism. Authors like Samuel Selvon, writing close to the time, created a comic persona which still stands in for the identity of Caribbeans in London – artful dodgers in an alien landscape, their difficulties outlined and defined by mutual ignorance. Over the past three decades events have intensified our focus on race, and on the other side of the coin, notions about culture became the medium of racial assertion during that period.

Selvon's people were exiles, dreaming of a species of paradise to which they imagined returning. I knew at the time that my dream was different. The pain of separation was as brief as it was intense, and what I wanted more than anything was to reinvent myself, and to construct a way of being at ease in my new surroundings. In any case, my experience of meeting London was never an encounter with a monolithic alien culture. For instance, the white boys and girls I met were as foreign as I was to the traditional ideas about 'Englishness', which was defined by a middle-class, public-school elite, and which was part of the language of the politicians and the newspapers. Our conflicts were outside such notions. Our geography of London was the opposite of the clutch of institutions and landmarks which housed the engines of power. We met and struggled, instead, over a space which was physical and material and in which we could be ourselves, whatever we thought that was. What happened between us was a rite of passage which bound us together rather than drove us apart, and in retrospect my choices all pointed in this direction.

More than forty years after my first year at school in North London, I had an unexpected encounter with a man who had been the notable leader of a gang of Teds around Holloway Road. I had been giving a reading at a book festival in Stoke Newington, and afterwards a middle-aged white woman approached me. She was married, she said, to one of the Teds I mentioned in my talk. They had read my books and, hearing me speak, her husband wanted to meet me to talk about the old days. It was an invitation I couldn't resist, and he turned out to be the prosperous and mild-mannered owner of a local pub, who remembered the year when he and his friends brought terror to the streets as a time of boyish pranks and harmless mischief.

I wanted to write novels almost from the time I started reading them. At first it was a vague, unrealizable fantasy, on a par with my desire to be a cowboy or to wear a sword like Zorro. In my mind writers were equally fabulous creatures who had died long ago, or who existed in a faraway landscape outside the reach of my experience; the books they had created were foreign objects, bringing messages from the real world of wars and aeroplanes, famous men and skyscrapers – a world where history existed and was made. My arrival in this world had been an unpredictable event, but once there, my ideas about being a writer hardened into certainty. On the other hand, I wanted to write about growing up in London, but the place where I had come to live seemed to have nothing to do with the city I had imagined. When I began thinking about how to describe my life in it, my certainties dissolved into confusion. For more than a decade after coming to Britain it was quite clear that I was a foreigner, an outsider whose presence was a historical accident to be, more or less, tolerated. In the circumstances I had no confidence that what I felt about London would make sense to anyone except myself, but my bewilderment was not simply internal. The other obstacle which stood in my way was London itself.

Almost two thousand years before I arrived, Boudicca, queen of the Iceni, had swept down from East Anglia to massacre, hang and crucify its inhabitants, followed up by burning the place to the ground. Her grasp of the political geography anticipated

London's imperialist role long before the city became the headquarters of the British Empire. But London's importance was never simply to do with administration. In the colonial periphery, and especially in the Caribbean, it was the image of London which shaped and focused concepts about Britain. This was an inevitable consequence of the exercise of imperial authority, and the operations of the state were accompanied by an imagery intended to transform the distant imperium into a routine aspect of our domestic imagination. London lurked in our language like a virus, carried on a stream of words and ideas which had acquired the power of myth, and I had always possessed a mental map of the city which sketched out an outline of its institutions – Buckingham Palace. The British Museum. The LSE. The MCC. Parliament. The Foreign Office. Scotland Yard. Somewhere there was also a capital city which was an upper-class playground, a financial centre, a gathering of intellectual giants and a forum of abstruse political debate. All these were landmarks in the London I knew before I set foot in its streets, but during my initial encounter with the city, they might as well have been operating on the moon. The London I lived in seemed to have a different history, and to be organized around different elements.

In comparison, the Caribbean writers to whom I turned in search of reinforcement seemed, disappointingly, stuck with the colonial eye's view of London which they had brought with them from Jamaica or Trinidad. Samuel Selvon's characters, for instance, move around the city as if blundering through a thicket of difficult and alien obstacles: its weather, its indifference, its hostility. The occasional story outlines random features as a backdrop to more agreeable experiences, but the London in Selvon's writing is a kind of absence, a wasteland which merely reflects his characters' sense of isolation and loneliness. In George Lamming's books London is less than a landscape, more an environment which can only be glimpsed through the filter of his characters' anguish. Whatever virtues these authors possessed, they offered little or no help in my confrontation with London. My relationship with the city had changed with every year I had spent in it, and by the end of the decade it was as if I had never belonged anywhere else. Instead I had begun to wrestle a sense of security from the routine business of living in it.

For example, during the Christmas holidays I worked in the Post Office, delivering letters and parcels. The centre from which we worked was a huge barn of a place near the Angel. It was called the Royal Agricultural Hall, but it was obviously a long time since anything either royal or agricultural had taken place there. In that sense it was typical of the way the city's buildings were always being converted to new uses. Sometimes the facades were preserved, sometimes it was a carving or a piece of sculpture, sometimes all that remained of their former identity was a memory. The RAH had a vaulted glass ceiling, which soared into the darkness of the morning. Inside, the floor was divided into a warren of stalls, each containing a clutch of huge postbags which gradually filled up with letters and parcels. When the bags were full we loaded them onto the vans and drove them through the streets. After a week I knew my area like the back of my hand, and tramping up and down with my arms full of messages and gifts I felt knowledgeable and important. When I knocked on the doors people smiled or said good morning in a matter-of-fact way, as if my appearance was an unremarkable part of their day. In the darkness before dawn I got out of bed and hurried through the empty streets, buoyed up by a sense of pleasure and anticipation.

This experience was a watershed. Up to that point the streets, the houses and the white people I encountered had seemed mysterious and unknowable. Now I saw them through different eyes.

My intentions didn't change, however, and the first person I told about my desire to become a writer was my former schoolmate, Geoff. This was a couple of hours after midnight on the first day of 1964. We had been to a party near Kilburn, and on our way home we started talking about our plans for the future. In fact I had no plans, only a desperate wish. Geoff was different. On leaving school he had gone to work as a lab assistant in one of the faculties of the university, and within a couple of years he had started a science degree in Edinburgh. This was his first vacation, and he had come back full of stories about new things – his posh girlfriend, his visits to the countryside, his conversations with professors.

This was a shock to me. We had grown up together during our last years at school, and afterwards we were still close friends, but now he seemed a different person, whose conscious superiority made me feel inadequate and resentful. In this mood, and attempting to impress him, I invited Geoff to accompany me to a party hosted by someone I knew slightly, a nurse who had recently arrived from Guyana. The women there would be older and more sophisticated than ourselves, most of them in their early twenties, and since I already knew some of them, I would have an advantage. Seeing me shine in this company would, I hoped, shut him up about the glories of student life in Edinburgh.

Matters didn't turn out quite as I expected. Everyone there seemed to be a student from the Caribbean or Africa, and their talk was all about the politics back home or their prospects on returning. To these people, London was a temporary and inhospitable stopping place, whose coldness and animosity they repaid with dislike and contempt. Before long Geoff and I felt ourselves to be sharing the same sense of being outsiders in this crowd, fish out of water. Geoff, who was now more confident and clear-sighted than myself about what he intended to do, boldly declared to one of the girls that he had no intention of going back to Jamaica or anywhere in Africa. All that he knew about where he had come from, he said, was poverty and misery, and now he owed nothing to it. In a moment we were soon embroiled in one argument after another about our loyalties and about where we belonged. In the process we were both trying to express for the first time the strange idea that, somehow, we belonged in London.

Shortly after midnight it began to snow, thick flakes whirling down in a continuous shower which, within half an hour, covered the landscape with a layer of ice-cream white. Going through Kentish Town and down to Seven Sisters Road the snow shone in front of us, a white page, empty and unmarked. Behind us our footsteps made two straight furrows. After parting from Geoff I walked on through the white night feeling small and solitary. In any other circumstances weather like this would have made me want to stay indoors or wait for a lift, but leaving had seemed like the only possible escape from a maelstrom of confusion and misunderstanding. I had expected to find myself part of a group of people like myself, but there was no disguising the fact that Geoff and I were somehow different. Most of the other guests had been only a few years older, and they came from the same sort of background as myself. They were boys and girls whom I might have known as a child, but now it was as if a few years of separation had put an insuperable distance between us.

— 2 —

London, 1960 to 1970

After the riots in Notting Hill, experts on the radio and in the newspapers came up with a variety of reasons why they had happened,
which all came back to the same thing. There were too many black
Caribbeans crossing the borders. This was before 1960 when the
numbers of Afro-Caribbeans appearing in the streets seemed to be
multiplying with every day that passed. If I hadn't been able to see
it with my own eyes, it would have been easy to guess what was
happening from the angry and contemptuous tone of the letters in
our local papers, or the debates and speeches about limiting immigration proliferating in Parliament. Oddly enough, although the
hostility of public discussion about our presence had become more
and more intense, I felt increasingly confident and relaxed about
living in London. Whenever we talked to white people we knew
about the rage and hatred which surrounded us, they were likely to
say that it was all to do with the novelty of our sudden appearance.
White people weren't used to seeing us, they said, because, back in
the dawn of time, the population of the British Isles had always
been completely white. At first this seemed like an incontrovertible
truth, an appropriate focus for a network of racist arguments. Later
on, the more I discovered about the country and its capital, the more
apparent it became that the real truth was that blacks had been air-
brushed out of our social history. This fact struck me forcibly during
the early 1970s in Liverpool and Manchester, cities whose centres
were largely populated by thousands of people with dark skins and
African features. Walking around these areas for the first time, what
kept popping into my head was the fact that, although these

communities had flourished here for generations, all the debates about migration were framed within the consensus that Britain had been milk-white until we arrived in the mid-twentieth century.

In one sense this is no surprise, because history reinvents itself according to contemporary needs, but in hindsight, the extent to which black people are still invisible in London's history is startling. This is true for other parts of the country, but in London it's more surprising if only because, even in the 1950s, no one would have had to look very hard to uncover the tracks of London's black and African communities. There are any number of hints. Go as far back as Londinium and logic dictates the presence of Africans, who had long been finding their way into Europe through the medium of the Roman Empire. This is a speculation supported by recent archaeological finds, but after the sixteenth century there is no need for guesswork or archaeology, because there is a great deal of documentary evidence. Queen Elizabeth I took enough notice to fire off a series of angry letters about the 'divers blackamoors brought into these realms, of which kind there are already here to manie'. At the beginning of the seventeenth century she followed this up by issuing a Royal Proclamation ordering the 'blackamoors' out of the kingdom.

Almost two centuries later, the Jamaican planter Edward Long was bitterly lamenting 'the unnatural increase of blacks' in the country, and this is merely a highlight in a long trail of references, both literary and visual, which point to the pervasive presence of black people, as well as illustrating the extent to which they were noticed and discussed. The trail runs through the work of essayists, painters and cartoonists like Hogarth, through parish records and lists of poor relief, through the gossip of the town and the debates of the plantocracy and the Abolitionists.

In 1772, when Lord Chief Justice Mansfield ruled in favour of freedom for the former African slave James Somerset, a group of black Londoners were in court to applaud the verdict. Soon afterwards a black woman called Dido attended a dinner party at the judge's house, giving rise to nasty rumours about her influence on the ruling. Throughout the eighteenth and nineteenth centuries, leaving aside well-known writers and polemicists like Olaudah Equiano, Ottobah Cuguano or Ignatius Sancho, there were other black personalities who became routine elements of London life, for example Samuel Johnson's servant Francis Barber, whose name crops up in a wide variety of letters and diaries. In his life of Johnson, Christopher Hibbert quotes the Revd Noel Turner about one occasion when he encountered Frank in Dr Johnson's house. Opening the door to an anteroom, he discovered Barber with a 'group of his African countrymen sitting round the fire', and, 'on their all turning their sooty faces at once to stare at me, they presented a curious spectacle'.

From that time onwards almost every major historical event seems to have deposited black people in London. In the aftermath of the American War of Independence the black community around Paddington and Mile End was inflated by the thousands of blacks who had fought or collaborated with the British. Similarly, the vagaries of empire drew in large numbers of traders, soldiers and entertainers. From about the mid-eighteenth century a number of West Africans sent their sons to a church school in Clapham, which had been established specifically for that purpose. At the other end of the scale the journalist Henry Mayhew, in his famous portraits of London street life, repeatedly mentions various categories of black beggars, criminals and entertainers.

So London's streets and buildings are full of the ghosts of unsung blacks, but you could argue that the blacks are invisible in our history partly because the poor of the city were always more or less invisible. A repetitive theme of the city's life is the astonishment of the ruling elites when the poor break out of enclaves like St Giles', and set out to tear the house down.

Take the Gordon Riots, which now tend to be mentioned in accounts of London as a mere footnote about anti-Catholic sentiment in the eighteenth century. Of course, it is probably true that the riots were triggered by Lord George Gordon's fervid and populist opposition to the Catholic Relief Act, together with the march in support of the Protestant Association's petition. On the other hand, once the demonstration had begun, its extreme violence and destructiveness took on a character which would have been familiar to any Londoner. The crowds of respectable artisans and tradesmen, largely animated by their fear of Catholic rule, were soon replaced by fanatics, street boys, prostitutes, drunks, pickpockets and assorted rowdies whose whole intent was destruction. As the excitement grew more intense and the authorities abandoned any pretence of control, the mob attacked Newgate Prison, the city's most suffocating symbol of oppression. Again, the style of the attack is immediately recognizable.

> Many of these figures could be seen standing perilously, in postures of arrogant, abandoned recklessness, on ledges, the tops of walls and astride window-sills in those parts of the building not yet too hot to touch. Now hidden by gusts of black sulphurous smoke, now brightly lit in a cascade of sparks, they shouted obscenities at each other and made vulgar gestures as they urinated into the flames, seemingly unconscious of their danger or at least heedless of it. (Christopher Hibbert, *King Mob*)

These characters were aided and abetted by

> thousands upon thousands of ordinary poor working men and women and children, flowing out of the slums of Shoreditch, Spitalfields and St Giles' and the unpaved, unlit, decaying warrens of streets and courtyards down the river. Pale and forgotten people, ill, hollow-cheeked and hungry, they poured from the doss-houses, crowded cellars and workshops to watch the houses burning; to run forward to grab a leg of mutton from a larder, a bottle from a cellar, a scorched blanket from a bonfire. (*ibid.*)

Thousands of black Londoners lived in these same conditions, and among the leaders of the assault on Newgate were a number of black people. John Glover, who was, until the riots, a 'quiet, sober, honest man', struck the cobble-stones in Snow Hill with a gun barrel and bellowed, 'Now Newgate.' Lucy Gardiner led a mob to a publican's house near Tower Hill and encouraged them to burn it down: 'Well done my boys.' Along with several other blacks, they were publicly hanged for their pains.

So, at the end of the century, no one could have been in doubt that the city had an active and engaged black population. On the other hand, the ideology of the Victorian empire had to re-create a new image of the imperial capital, and its effects persisted well into the twentieth century.

In much the same way, the literature of the time employs an aggressive discretion about the existence and role played by black people in British life. This is not altogether surprising, since, even in the late eighteenth century, the contradiction between Christian ethics and human property could be bridged only by a systematic hypocrisy. Jane Austen, for instance, has one of her most virtuous characters in *Mansfield Park* going off to examine his property in Barbados, and I read the book more than once before it struck me that any business in which he was engaged on the island had to involve sugar plantations and slaves.

The Brontë sisters, by comparison, were always much more self-aware and honest writers, and were correspondingly more committed to picking up the undercurrents which were shaping imperial ideology about race. In *Jane Eyre*, Charlotte's creation of Mr Rochester's mad wife draws on the biological racism which underlay the West Indian settlers' arguments about the pathology of blackness and the dangers of miscegenation. The implications of 'tainted blood' were straightforward and devastating. Her sister Emily, a deeper and more imaginative thinker, turns the theme on its head in *Wuthering Heights*. She drops a few hints about Heathcliff's origins. He is picked up on the streets in Liverpool; that is, precisely the district notorious for its mixed-race population. She gives her readers another clue by describing him as probably 'the son of a Lascar', Lascar being the popular term for African and Indian seamen. Using a combination of the supernatural and her own internal rage and confusion, she creates Heathcliff as something more than an outsider figure. The story is an acutely insightful pre-diction of psychoanalytic arguments about the role of race in the imagination. Heathcliff is both the enemy and the temptation of the soul, the eternal Other.

Remarkably, all these manifestations of black British life struck me as a surprisingly familiar assembly of opposing elements. Black lives were hidden and marginalized, but at the same time black people could play a leading part in shaping popular movements. The existence of blacks was ignored in the elite councils of the culture, but at the same time blacks and blackness animated the creativity of writers and artists. Black people were absent or downgraded in the conduct of politics and society, while at the same time being perceived as a continuing menace to order.

Uncovering these remains of black life in Britain and in the capital was like an archaeological task in which I had to dig through layers of oblique awareness. But there was also no doubt that life in London was clearly marked by the tracks of black predecessors a long time before post-war migration began, and a long time before I began to think about such things. Reading their meaning was another matter.

It was no accident, however, that the reassessment of this aspect of British history gathered momentum in the decade of the 1960s. This was the time when, within the span of about ten years, London's role as the capital of the Empire evaporated, and the city began to struggle with its new post-imperial identity. Ironically, the popular imagery which sums up 1960s London, driven by television's lust for simple and dramatic pictures, focuses on fashion and on a few major events, such as CND's anti-nuclear marches or student demonstrations against the Vietnam War. All this, however, was mere froth on the crest of waves. The significant changes in the fabric and the self-image of the city were animated by a series of battles over industrial power and authority in the workplace, by the anguish associated with a cyclone of decolonization and by the political ferment around the issue of migration. For the bulk of Londoners the period was marked by the continuing arrival of Afro-Caribbeans in the city, followed by waves of Asians from Africa and the subcontinent. Accompanying this movement was the continuous irritation of transport strikes or housing shortages, and the trauma of Powellism, all of them object lessons which prompted the sense that the city was going through a process of fundamental and unstoppable change.

For the first few years of the 1960s I had the sense that I was living in the eye of a storm, which may have been something to do with the fact that I was seeing the city from the safety of my first job as an assistant in my local public library. Somehow I had gravitated to the only place within my reach where reading was a legitimate activity and I could read as much as I wanted. It was meant to be a temporary job during which I would decide what I wanted to do, and I had the vague intention of applying for a university course during the following year. Instead I stayed for four years. Part of the reason was the books. On my first day, as I walked through the building, I was struck by the idea that everything I wanted to know about the world was somewhere on the shelves around me. With the naivety and optimism of adolescence I followed up this insight by deciding to read the complete works of every famous author in the world. I started near the top of the alphabet with Balzac, but before long my system broke down and I was reading whatever caught my eye. In the process, the job and its routines had become a sort of cocoon. Even now, walking into a library brings an instant recollection of the murmuring silence, the smell of wax polish, the dusty patina the books left on my hands, and I can see myself travelling home with a bundle of books under my arm.

The sheer comfort of the situation also had something to do with my fellow workers. Apart from the librarian and her deputy, who were two middle-aged women, my colleagues were all about the same age as myself. Alan Page, now a well-known artist and still a friend, joined the library after completing his National Service, and he had the self-contained and slightly intimidating confidence I associated with having been a soldier, but he had attended the same school as I had, so we had an immediate connection. One of the other boys was the son of a famous London comedian, Tony Hancock's sidekick Arthur Mullard, and with hardly any provocation he'd while away a couple of hours going through his dad's routines. All the others came from the familiar neighbourhood in which we worked. A couple of them were, like me, recent school leavers, and during our breaks we invented nicknames for the readers, talked about our prospects of salary increases, argued about the rock 'n' roll charts and discussed books. What we had in common apart from our age was the fact that we had all grown up in London within a stone's throw of each other, and we were all mad about books. In the circumstances it would have been difficult not to get interested in the process of writing, and looking back at the experience it was probably inevitable that I would go on to study literature, but, for the moment, a formal education seemed irrelevant. For the first time I had discovered a space in the city where I felt secure, unassailable, and it was another two years before I began to think about leaving. My eventual rescue was something to do with my distant ambition to be a writer, or, to be more precise, it was to do with Joe Orton.

Orton and his friend Kenneth Halliwell came into the building practically every day, but it was Orton whom we liked, because he had a friendly mischievous air, and he always made some kind of humorous comment as he went in and out. I had no idea then that he was going to be a famous writer, and no one knew, of course, that this pair were smuggling out books, which they carefully vandalized before returning them. Their handiwork had been cropping up for months without our knowing who was responsible. They specialized in making obscene alterations to reproductions of classic paintings. On the figure of Christ on the Cross in a Giotto, for example, an enormous penis would appear, while a cut-out Madonna or angel would be posed so that their lips pressed against it. Alternatively, the blurb on the jacket of some innocuous bestseller would be covered over by a painstakingly typed fake, outlining a story of strange and disgusting perversions. The authorities ignored their activities until members of the public began complaining, then the police were duly notified, and within a short time the confident vandals were arrested, convicted of stealing and defacing public property, and sentenced to prison.

The event caused an enormous stir in our small world. The consensus among older and wiser heads was that the couple, motivated by envy and frustration, had got what they deserved. The real climax of the story, however, only came when we heard that Orton had written a successful play which was shortly to go into production. The news had a galvanic effect on me. At the time of his trial, hearing about his frustrated desire to be a writer, I had been intrigued and disturbed by the fact that, without knowing it, we shared the same hopeless dreams. In spite of myself, I couldn't help identifying with his downfall. His conviction and imprisonment had seemed like the end of his ambitions, and, for me, it was an evil and depressing omen.

By the time the rumours about *Entertaining Mr Sloane* began to circulate I was already bored and desperate, because the cosy embrace of the library had begun to seem like imprisonment. In comparison, Orton had exiled himself from the verities of small-town life. Ironically, I had no idea at the time that he was a homosexual, and I assumed that the way he lived was somehow a symptom of his commitment as a writer. It was obvious, too, that his play was a destructive attack not only on suburban hypocrisy, but also on the literary tradition which confronted him. His favourite targets had been authors like Godfrey Winn and Beverley Nichols, the cloying idols of the middle-aged ladies who made up the bulk of our clientele, and, on reflection, everything he had done seemed both rational and heroic. He had used the only outlet available to confront and attack tradition or hypocrisy, and when they caught him, he hadn't given up. Instead he had raised the stakes and escaped by writing himself into history. He was the only writer whom I was conscious of encountering in my adult life up to that point, and to all appearances he was an ordinary young guy like myself. If he could do it, I thought, I could do no less. In the year that *Entertaining Mr Sloane* had its first production, I applied to enter a degree course in English, and shook the dust of the library from my feet.

Half-way through the 1960s I was an undergraduate and living in my own flat in Tottenham, when my parents announced they were emigrating to the USA. Their decision took me by surprise, part of which, I suppose, was to do with the fact that, in comparison with the previous decade, London seemed safer, more manageable, more like our home. In the half-dozen years since the riots, the stream of incoming Caribbeans had created enclaves in areas like Notting Hill and Brixton which were focal points of migrant life. Unlike the time when we first arrived there were now places to go and people to see. In the time my parents had spent in London they had also built up a wide circle of friends and acquaintances. Their house, in a friendly, moderately prosperous area, was more spacious than they needed.

My father, now well established in his job with the Post Office, was becoming a figure in the local Labour Party. In the isolation of the previous decade it would have seemed logical and sensible to leave. Ten years later, their decision seemed perverse. But I had reckoned without my mother's feelings. She had never ceased to grieve for my brother, and for her being in London was a constant reminder of failure and loss. On the other hand, she was a stoical, self-contained person, less emotional and outgoing than my father, and she might have simply remained in the same situation if it hadn't been for her Aunt Muriel.

Aunt Muriel had migrated to the USA as a teenager, back in 1923. Until my mother went to visit her forty years later, I never quite believed that she was real. She was a mere name to us, a family legend, like my mother's father Joe, who had departed when she was a child, carrying only his clarinet, with which he intended to make his fortune in Harlem. No one ever heard from Joe again, but Muriel turned out to be alive and well and flourishing in New York. She had lived since the 1920s in a huge brownstone off Amsterdam Avenue, and when my mother went to stay there she was immediately seduced by the prospect which opened up in front of her. Apart from anything else, she had been relieved to be out of London, and once again part of her extended family. When she came back from New York the first time, her eyes were shining, and she was more animated than I'd seen her for a long time. The following year when she went to see Aunt Muriel, she took my father with her. After that it was only a matter of time. The worst part of their disappearance was that all the other members of my family seemed to vanish at the same time. My eldest sister accompanied my parents to New York. Another sister's husband went back to Guyana where he'd found the sort of a job he wanted. My youngest sister finished her last year at school and, horrified by the prospects facing her, also found a job in Guyana and promptly left. It was as if by waving her hand my mother had dispersed us all, and suddenly I was alone in London.

I had spent a few weeks thinking about whether I should go with them. I had a good reason for staying. After all, I was half-way through a university degree. On the other hand, even if that had not been the case, I would have refused to leave London. When I thought about the prospect a mood of stubborn defiance came over me. It wasn't so much that I loved London: I couldn't quite believe that, but I had invested so much emotion and energy in the city that to leave would be like abandoning part of myself. My parents had given up rather more, but I already knew why their feelings about the matter were so different. They hadn't migrated simply for work or adventure. Those things had moved them, but at the root of their actions was the belief that they could transform themselves. We had come from a rootless, landless group of people whose only capital was their own potential, and the lust to better themselves burned as fiercely in my parents' hearts as when they had first set out. London had depressed them and undermined their self-belief. Even worse, the city seemed to offer them no further possibilities for change or advancement. Preparing to leave, they seemed happier and more optimistic about the future than they had for years.

I tried to share their excitement, but it was hard to imagine what sort of life they would lead. Before London I had been protected by my sheer ignorance of the place. In comparison, I knew enough about the USA to be fearful and depressed. The British media were full of American conflicts. On television we saw the progress of the civil rights movement, the murders of black men, the assassinations of the Kennedys and Martin Luther King. Black life in the USA seemed dangerous and embattled, but when I talked to them about such matters my parents merely smiled and told me there was no need to worry. Unlike hypocritical London, they said, the lines were clearly drawn in the USA. You knew where you were.

Listening to them, I felt a complex mixture of anger and admiration at their refusal to accept the limitations of age, politics or geography. Would I ever be able, I wondered, to live up to their courage? Both of them were already over 50, and with more than half their lives behind them my parents had set out again, into the unknown, buoyed up by the hope of better things to come.

I graduated the following year. Almost immediately I found myself among the ranks of the unemployed and homeless, and I began to acquire a new sort of knowledge about the city. The tunnels and gateways in the Underground were the best places for a night's sleep, for instance. The new Victoria Line was the earliest to open its stations, about half-past five in the morning, and you could get a couple of hours' sleep, riding up and down the line before the rush-hour started. Desperate, I signed up for some of the sort of jobs only vagrants and migrants could be persuaded to do, the most unpleasant jobs in the capital. These were notable for being crushingly repetitive or dangerously polluted. For example, I worked on the assembly line in a toy factory which made dartboards. When the completed dartboard arrived at my bench, I dipped the bull's-eye, a small plug of red wood, in glue and stuck it into a hole in the middle of the board. I did this over and over again for eight hours until it was time to go home. After this I worked as an undersealer's mate. We stood in a dark pit, filled with fumes and dripping chemicals, spraying a stream of cars as they flowed overhead. In a short while I'd be light-headed and dizzy as my lungs filled up with the fumes. Even after I climbed out of the pit it was impossible to get rid of the smell, and at night I collapsed into muttering nightmares. After this I worked in a series of factories, humping bits of sharp-edged metal around, then in a hospital for geriatric epileptics where most of the patients were incontinent, and then in a number of garages where I pumped petrol and fiddled with engines. Finally, I came to rest in the Post Office's international telephone exchange, putting through calls to France and Spain.

In this new position, the differences in my working life were amazing. I had frequent breaks, and I spent half the time chatting to my colleagues. I could take sick-leave, and I had a pension. In this new atmosphere the realization hit me that it was largely my own ineptitude that had confined me to the lowest-paid, unskilled and dirty end of the job market. I knew, of course, that part of it had been the fact that the colour of my skin cancelled out my qualifications, and I was effectively barred from the sort of white-collar occupations my former classmates were taking up. In the market for semi-skilled and better-paid jobs I was 'over-qualified'. Even so, the truth was that I had given up and tamely joined a group of workers who had no choice.

Years later, and against all expectations, I found myself looking back with satisfaction on the perspective from which I had seen the city. While I had been working in these sites, they had actually been in the process of disappearing. The toy factory and the hospital closed down within a year of my leaving. The garages where six of us worked the night shift became self-service. Within a few years the miserable army of low-paid workers had shifted from the lowest rungs of the industrial ladder to fast-food outlets, minicabs, cleaning firms and sweatshops. One thing didn't change. These jobs were no help in establishing bank loans and overdrafts, or generating mortgages. People in this kind of work were the downwardly mobile who might at any moment double as beggars or thieves or dope peddlers.

Ironically, the city couldn't function without this fringe of insecure and marginal labourers. No one else would do this work at the price. Without them the organism would have ground to a halt, and, just as it had been for centuries, it was part of the city's self-serving function to maintain them in their vulnerable status, so as to deliver them up where and when they were needed.

In comparison, my fellow workers at the Post Office had something to defend. In the nationalized industries and all the other big firms a long history of conflict or negotiation had created a class of workers who had mortgages, cars and families, protected by their regular salaries, pensions, sick-pay and various benefits. In secure workplaces of this kind Powellism was rampant, and the decade was marked by a series of long and bitter battles to halt the incursion of migrants. While I worked at the Post Office the racist National Front was a dominant voice in the union's affairs. Powell's speeches attacking blacks and urging migrant repatriation added to their strength, and it took a protracted struggle within the union before they were expelled from its leadership.

As it happened, the privileged unionized workplaces were changing as rapidly as the world in which the peripatetic and unskilled workers were confined. By the end of the decade the skilled workforces in the light engineering factories, the Post Office and the railways had begun to contract. The local landmarks of my youth, like the tobacco-packing plant in Camden Town, the Metal Box factory, and a plethora of light engineering firms, disappeared almost overnight.

These had been the strongholds at the heart of London, and they had moved and shaped its population for longer than anyone could remember. As they faded away, old Londoners complained incessantly about how much the city had been transformed. Throughout the 1970s they continued to conduct a bitter and often vicious rearguard battle against the newcomers, but by the end of the decade the bulk of the old industries had accelerated the move they'd been making since the end of the war, outwards to other parts of the country, or around the fringes of London. They took their workforces with them, complete with their networks, their customs and their nationalistic claims to ownership of the city. London's roots were loosening and changing, leaving the way open for the city to be shaped in a new image.

— 3 —

New York, 1970

The next time I saw my mother and father was in July 1970. When they left London I had half expected never to see them again, because I understood that Britain had been an interlude in their lives, and once they were settled in New York I knew instinctively that they would see no point in retracing their footsteps. On my side, going there to visit them seemed like a giant undertaking. It involved passports, visas and a long flight over the Atlantic. I knew no one who undertook such trips casually, and I had become accustomed to thinking about my parents as part of a life which was in the past. In any case, it had taken me a long time to conquer my anger about the dispassionate style of their departure. This wasn't because I imagined that they had no concern for me. Instead, my emotions were an echo of what I had felt when they had left Guyana, the occasion of our first separation. Something about that time had altered our relationship irrevocably. When they left London it was as if they had abandoned me a second time.

I knew that I was being unreasonable about this, because I also understood that the strains which migration put on our lives had defined the possibilities. In London we were forced to become individuals, developing autonomous relationships outside the family circle in a way which, beforehand, would have been unthinkable. Each one of us had our own problems to solve, and somehow our mutual expectations made things worse. The rituals which gave our family life a shape and purpose had disappeared when we crossed the ocean. For example, we had all attended church services every Sunday, but my parents' church-going had been a matter of habit and social custom rather than passionate conviction, and faced with the hostility or indifference of English fellow Christians they had simply stopped going. So, in London, stepping outside the door meant that we each disappeared into a different milieu where we were alone and where we had to adapt ourselves to differing requirements. After a time, it seemed, we were strangers bound together only by necessity and the past.

Something else separated us. Few of the migrants from our region foresaw how drastic the effects of living in Britain would be on their children. If my parents had a dream for me, it was that I would acquire the esoteric qualifications which would propel me into the ranks of the professional classes, and my ideal future would be one in which I would be prosperous and secure, free of the necessities of their own lives.

In London, it must have seemed to them, I had rejected all my opportunities for advancement and embraced the shiftless, insecure style of life from which they had worked so hard to free themselves, and which had swallowed up my brother. When I tried seeing it through their eyes, it was clear that the process of becoming a Londoner was also a process in which I was rejecting aspects of my own past. It was precisely those aspects of myself that, at the time, were most important to them.

As I got off the plane, the heat floated off the tarmac and hit me like a blast from a furnace. Outside the terminal I found myself wondering what they would be like and whether they would be glad to see me. I found myself reliving the feelings of fear and expectation I had experienced fifteen years before on the boat approaching Southampton. It had been colder then than I had ever imagined, and tears had sprung into my eyes the moment that I saw them, bulky and strange in their overcoats. Now, when I got off the plane and walked into the incredible heat, the contrast with that freezing day long ago struck me immediately, and, in much the same way, this meeting was to be the opposite of that other time.

Everything about my parents seemed to have gone through another set of unpredictable changes. The first surprise was to see my father behind the wheel of a car. He had never owned one before, and until then I didn't know he could drive. His appearance was also very different from the way I remembered. Before leaving London he had been ill and harassed. Now he was wearing a loose white shirt with a snap-brim straw hat in which he looked cool and prosperous, his manner relaxed and jovial. My mother and older sister, who had also come to meet me, seemed to have gone through the same sort of changes, because they had acquired a sleek, groomed air. In the old days I would have guessed that they were wearing their best clothes and going out somewhere special, but it was soon obvious that this was now their routine style.

In the car we talked, hugging each other repeatedly. The uncertainty I experienced had disappeared in a moment, and nagging in my mind was the strange feeling that they were more like their old selves, the people they had been before we met in London. My father had a new list of jokes and stories. I told him how well he looked, and he received the compliment with a complacent grin.

Their house was in Queens, not far from the airport. After the dingy basement in Notting Hill where I lived, it seemed palatial. There was no doubt about it. In the five years since they had left London their fortunes had changed, and they had become Americans, with everything that entailed. I understood later that the way they had established themselves was a product of their previous life. Selling their house in London had given them the capital to buy one in New York, and my mother's aunt had already possessed the experience and contacts which smoothed their path. Even so, the transformation seemed to sum up some quality about the city to which they had come. For people as experienced and energetic as my parents, it had been relatively easy.

My father kept on surprising me. I went to lunch with him the following day. Before I left the house my mother rummaged through my clothes, and then went out and bought me a new jacket and a pair of trousers. 'You can't go up there looking like that,' she told me, and by that time I was too psyched out to argue.

My father now had an administrative job at Columbia University. Leaving his office, we walked up Broadway to a restaurant, where we spent a couple of hours talking about what had happened to him. The first time he met Aunt Muriel, he told me, she had said that he looked so fine he ought to be a preacher. 'All you need is the first six women,' she added. He had taken the remark as a clue about the nature of the place he was in. Appearances were everything. So was greed. 'These are the greediest people on God's earth,' he said. 'Those are the only things you need to understand about this city.' Following the money, he entered a course in accountancy, and turned out to be in the right place at the right time. His appearance and accent convinced everyone of his trustworthiness, and after signing up for a temporary bookkeeping job at Columbia, he had been rapidly promoted to a post as treasurer of an academic foundation. Now he evaluated research programmes, signed cheques for a list of scholars and worked with celebrities like Averell Harriman. 'They look at me,' he said slyly, 'and they see an educated man.' Moved by the sense that we were talking together as adults for the first time, I told him that it didn't matter, that what he had was more important than an armful of degrees, but he shook his head with a hint of sadness. 'No I'm not. Not like you.'

The fact was, however, that he had fetched up in a place where remaking oneself was the project of most lives. It had been like starting with a clean sheet, on which it was possible to rewrite both past and future, so it seemed as if my parents lived in a bright new bubble. This was an impression reinforced by the arrival from Guyana of my remaining two sisters and my younger brother. My sisters had come to stay, while for my brother it was a stage during which he would make a choice between the colleges which had offered to admit him. We were now reunited for the first time in years, and, in retrospect, it was a bright, joyful summer. All my fears about the city had evaporated and it seemed full of delight and sweet sounds. Unlike London we already had two generations of friends and family living close at hand. They had migrated to the USA over the past fifty years, and now they welcomed us with open arms. Aunt Muriel seemed to know everyone and everything in Harlem. Every time I went to see her she would introduce me to a young woman, and, as I left, slip a sheaf of dollars into my pocket.

She was a passionate fan of the Mets and she took me to Shea Stadium to see the games, where she bought me a Mets hat and solemnly instructed me in the ritual of the seventh inning stretch. Another cousin owned a restaurant bar in Harlem. He was also a dentist and a part-time preacher, and, it was rumoured, a bit of a gangster.

During that summer we existed in a tightly constrained, heavily protected circle. Apart from my father's colleagues at work, all my parents' friends were from Guyana, and they formed a defensive and exclusive network, within which they shared benefits and profits. For the moment, however, this aspect of their lives wasn't clear to me. Anything and everything seemed possible. In fact, we had arrived at one of the happier episodes in the history of the city. President Johnson's concept of a Great Society had delivered a network of opportunities to a segment of the black population, the bedrock of the burgeoning black middle class, and they had given the city an optimistic, stylish bustle. 'Don't whistle walking down the street in Harlem,' my cousin Enid told me with a straight face, 'or some guy will grab you and shove a grant in your pocket.'

That was how it seemed, anyway. One of our first family outings, for instance, had been to a park in Queens to see the Public Theater's version of *The Two Gentlemen of Verona*. It was an evening performance, but the park was crowded with black people from around Jamaica Avenue and the housing project at Rochester Village. Everyone laughed and cheered, and we walked home in the dark without a qualm. A few years later the same park had become dangerous and menacing, but during that year it felt like a safe, relaxed environment.

After that, in an attempt to escape from the family circle, I began going to the theatre. Harlem and the Village seemed full of black performers operating in little halls and shop fronts. The Elks Hall near Aunt Muriel's house featured plays by such writers as Ed Bullins, LeRoi Jones and Archie Shepp. During the day I sometimes followed the Last Poets' truck into the amphitheatres created by the courtyards of housing projects. Around them the crowds shuffled and jostled, and up above their audience leaned out of the windows and balconies yelling and applauding. When they delivered lines like 'the revolution will not be broadcast on television', the whole place seemed to explode.

Attending these performances and watching the audiences, it was clear to me that my relatives had somehow short-circuited the conventional experience and expectations of black people in the city. To my family, it seemed, the issues of race and the discrimination associated with the colour of their skins were, more or less, inconveniences, or obstacles which could be circumvented by employing the appropriate techniques or strategies. By the same token, they regarded the psychological implications which bedevilled their African-American neighbours as self-imposed handicaps. They understood clearly that it was the vitality and passion of the African-Americans, people among whom they lived but about whom they knew little, which gave them the space to flourish, and gave life in New York a richness and texture it was impossible to imagine in London. At the same time, their self-interest forced them to maintain a distance from the communal struggle within which the Americans embraced each other; and it was this distance which made it possible for them to be so fulfilled and contented in the city.

If I lived there, I knew it would be impossible to keep my distance, but even so, I hesitated about returning to London. My young brother had already made his decision. Rejecting MIT and an athletic scholarship in Miami, without, it seemed, more than a moment's thought, he had opted to go to Imperial College in London.

'Don't go to London,' I advised him. 'It's a tough place.'

In reply, he shrugged and smiled.

'I was born there.'

Everyone I met gave me the same advice. Day after day they urged me to stay, and told me how good my prospects would be, and remembering how I felt then, it's still hard to understand why I came back to London.

— 4 —

London, 1970 to 1974

During the early years of the 1970s I visited the USA several times, and each time I thought seriously about staying. Paradoxically, while the idea of sharing the life of my relatives and friends attracted me, the thought of living near my parents made it impossible. Every conversation with my father, for example, seemed to include a reference to some rising young black academic, and although I suspected he was trying to somehow inspire me, his eulogies made me feel inadequate and irritable. The other problem was that my desire to write had been reawakened by everything I had seen in New York. On the other hand, the playwrights and poets I admired all wrote from the vantage point of their own heritage, and within an idiom which had been shaped by their own experience and history. Being able to write in that place would mean learning a new language which would perhaps never be mine.

In any case, the longer I hesitated, the more it seemed that London was where I wanted to be. The strange thing was that at the moment I had begun to consider leaving, I had also begun to discover something new in London. Blackness had suddenly become part of our public life. Of course, there was nothing sudden about it. The Notting Hill riots, followed by the furore of colonial independence, had undermined the easy complacency of imperialist racism in the city, but that had been replaced by a home-grown version, filtered through Powellism, and revolving around the issue of migration. The legislation which limited and then halted black and Asian immigration as the 1960s progressed began to change the nature of the argument. By the start of the 1970s, the issue of race ceased to focus on guarding the borders from the incursion of 'alien' blacks and began to be discussed in terms of how to live with the black migrants already in the country.

On the other side of the coin migrants were developing a new grip on their surroundings. Up to this point the relationship of most Afro-Caribbeans to the rest of the population had been more or less defensive. The ease with which my parents had left London was characteristic. They hated the aura of hostility and contempt which attached itself to us, but they couldn't dispute its origins. As they saw it, the city belonged to the English, and trying to dispute its owner-ship was a waste of time. In this environment their main objective was to defend themselves and take advantage of any opportunities which might open up. In comparison I was finding London almost intolerable precisely because I felt that I belonged in it, but paradox-ically there was nothing about its history, its institutions or its self-image which reflected my presence. This was a feeling shared by most of the other young Caribbeans who had grown up in the city during the previous decades. We knew instinctively that expressing this sense of belonging would involve the confrontation our parents had avoided. What we lacked was a medium.

The era of blackness in the USA seemed to show us a direction. Tele-vision gave us a long line of black spokesmen – Dr King, Malcolm X, the Panthers, Muhammed Ali – all of them distinguished by their colour and grounded by their roots. On the other hand, although it was easy to mimic their language and manners, their style remained irre-ducibly alien. In London, the idiom which had empowered the African-Americans became the tool of crooks and charlatans. Grasping for some link with this new identity, we saw people whom we'd known for years suddenly breaking into American accents, and we read about local Black Power adherents, like Michael X, who turned out to be mad and rotten. Even the language was deceptive. When the Americans talked about 'the ghetto' they were referring to districts where you could tour around for hours without seeing a white person. In London a 'black' district was one where there were a few more black faces than usual. By the end of the 1960s it was clear that if there was a way of being black in London we would have to create it ourselves.

At the start of the 1970s I was training to be a teacher at Goldsmiths College and working in a youth club in Neasden. The club was a house which was due to be demolished or renovated by the local council, and while it was standing empty they let us use it for the activities of the club. That was characteristic of the way we were carving out a public life from the fragments we could salvage. The boys and girls who came to the club were in early adolescence. The fact that they were coming together for any reason was remarkable enough, because their parents all came from different countries – Jamaica, St Lucia, Trinidad, Barbados and Guyana. Growing up in London, the power of those origins which had defined their parents' identities had faded and become rhetorical. What linked them now was the trauma of migration and the colour of their skins. A typical cross-section of young black people in the district, they went on to follow a wide variety of careers. One of them, Courtney Pine, became a famous musician. Another became a local entrepreneur. Another went in for armed robbery, his best friend became a university lecturer, and one of the cleverest and most vital of the lot died of stab wounds on a pavement in Battersea. We didn't do much except sit around, talk and organize parties, but what began to emerge in the circle of boys and girls around the club was a distinctive style which was being duplicated all over the city. The essential element was Jamaican music. Bob Marley is the best-known musician of that period, but his style and his music encapsulated a network of features shared by all cultural products coming out of the Caribbean, especially Jamaica.

In the aftermath of independence the Caribbean had begun to discover itself, and it was clear that racial oppression, along with the grinding poverty of the black majority, had outlived the end of colonialism. Caribbeans already had a precedent for linking their own condition with that of the black diaspora. Marcus Garvey had preached blackness and African roots in the USA as far back as the 1920s, and the religion he inspired, Rastafarianism, had become a seed-bed of ideas about our history and identity. For young black people brought up in London, there was no contradiction about adopting the style and language sweeping Jamaica. In contrast, up to that point, the idiom of the London streets had been the idiom of the enemy, and adopting it had been a kind of surrender. When we seized on Jamaican heroes like Marley, Toots and Big Youth, it was as if we were reinventing ourselves and describing what we were in a language that was exclusively ours.

At the same time, new avenues into the operations of the city had opened up. The youth club in which I worked was partly a response to the fact that there were now thousands of young black people in London, who were excluded, or had shut themselves off, from the social life of their white schoolfriends. A decade before the riots of 1981 their potential terrified the local authorities and social services, and towards the end of the previous decade new regulations had been enacted which allowed local councils to fund projects organized by local communities. The result was that a rash of clubs, community or advice centres, bookshops and hostels sprang up all over the city, which provided rallying points and refuges for young black people. Their rationale was the now familiar constituents of blackness – African roots, black history, the solidarity of colour and anti-racism – all of which had been taken apart and rearranged along domestic lines.

As it happened, the organizations which were crucial in re-creating these home-grown ideas about our identity were, at the time, a secular version of the black churches which had begun springing up with the growth of the Caribbean population. At first, people held services in their living rooms, then in back rooms loaned by friendly white congregations or spaces rented in a public building. Soon the black congregations began buying their own property or taking over white churches in the inner city where the congregation had dwindled to nothing. In much the same way, most of the 'self-help' projects were grouped around some charismatic black individual and backed up their ideology by shrewd dealing combined with the offer of some necessary service to the local community.

Necessity had been the source of our reinvention. The music, the black-run organizations, the churches, and the social life which went with them, were both expressions of our own identity and essential tools of survival. Some of the issues which had begun to emerge in the life of the Caribbean community seemed to concern only ourselves, and even when the authorities who ran the city noticed that we had a problem, they didn't seem to know what to do about it or to care enough to solve it. For instance, in this period, the first big campaign undertaken by the network we had begun to establish was on behalf of the black schoolchildren who throughout the previous decade had been categorized as educationally subnormal (ESN) by the education system and relegated to special schools and classes. Their numbers exceeded, by a long way, the proportion of white schoolchildren who found themselves in the same circumstances, and black parents, who had at first been disposed to accept all the system's judgements without question, began to protest. Fresh from a course in education I found myself teaching in a black Saturday school and helping black parents to challenge their schools' assessments of their children. Before long I was living in a commune with a group of black teenagers, fundraising and teaching by day, touring the clubs and handing out legal advice by night.

The house in which I lived was itself a response to another problem thrown up by the solidarity which was appearing in answer to the discrimination we faced. Throughout the 1960s Caribbean children had been the responsibility of their families, and in any case, for a while the migrants had been overwhelmingly adult and male. Suddenly, in the next decade, black children had begun to emerge from the 'care and protection' of local authorities. There were children who had found their way from the Caribbean or from all over Britain looking for parents who had abandoned them or somehow forgotten their existence. There were children who were orphans or whose parents had disappeared into gaol or mental hospitals. Expelled at the age of 16 from the hostels and foster homes where they lived, they swiftly lost any grip they might have had on conventional life, and soon found themselves homeless, wandering aimlessly around the city, ripe for induction into petty crime, prostitution or the growing drug industry.

The social services should have taken up the slack, but, demoralized by black challenges to their competence in dealing with the problems of young black people, they began appealing for the support of the black communities.

Ten years before this, the request would have fallen upon deaf ears. Caribbeans in London had been separated by national origin, their political interests focused on the island where they'd come from. Their loyalties were largely isolated within their own circles of family and friends, and generally they would have seen other people's children as unfortunate but none of their concern, especially when their parents came from another country. Now the atmosphere had changed. A variety of influences – Powellism, the discrimination they shared, and the sense that something new was on the way – had begun to persuade the Caribbeans that the colour of their skins implied a responsibility to other black people. When we lobbied the local council for a house and began offering shelter to homeless young blacks we were confident that the community of migrants in the district shared our aims. We were also naively confident that if the young drifters' lives lacked anything, it was a firm connection with other black people. Facing the local politicians and social workers, I argued boldly that since they couldn't help these young people their most sensible course was to back activists like myself.

The other influence which had forced solidarity on Caribbeans in London at this time was a fire-storm of police harassment. We called it 'suss', which referred to the legislation that allowed policemen to stop and search or take you in 'on suspicion'. The ever-present threat the police presented drew the black population together because, after a while, everyone knew what it felt like to be harassed, insulted and threatened by a cop, it didn't matter whether you were a thief, a mugger, a church sister on the way home or a university graduate on the way to work.

All these elements were coming together at the same time to create a politics of blackness in Britain which wasn't focused around history or religion or the prospect of a separate nation. Instead, it revolved around what was happening to us in cities like London, especially London, and around the way we were reshaping the spaces in which we lived.

A characteristic example of how the process worked was the

Notting Hill Carnival. When I first encountered the festival in the mid-1960s it was a scattered collection of processions, organized by the minority of Trinidadians who lived around the district. It had the air, in that period, of a slightly pathetic folk festival, a fading reminder of distant customs. During the first years of the 1970s, however, all the elements which were redefining our identity came together within the Carnival. The district already housed a constituency based on clubs, centres and communes like mine, which had been relentlessly watched, searched and raided by the local police. The festival was a Caribbean thing, and like the myriad 'self-help' projects, it was founded and run by black people. The warren of streets and houses around Notting Hill and Ladbroke Grove could also accommodate the Jamaican-inspired industry of clubs, DJs and sound systems, which had its centre in West London. The potential drew thousands of young black people into the area during the weekend of the Carnival, and their presence transformed it into a site of protest. For a few years the annual Carnival riot became a ritual, with boys and girls turning up from all over London to stone the police or loot the shops or just to watch the fun. The excitement they created drew in a wide swathe of the black population from every district in the city and beyond, because whatever else the Carnival was, it was also, first and foremost, about us. For a few days an entire quarter of London was our theatre and no one could stop it, but the violent annual disturbances that occurred throughout the 1970s were not a product of the Carnival. At that time Notting Hill was still full of crumbling, overcrowded houses and unemployed or low-paid transients, and the conditions had, since 1958, created militant pressures for change. During the early 1970s, the festival simply gathered up and reflected our rage. This was the only method we had of drawing attention to our discontent, and it gave the drama of our confrontation with London its most extreme and concrete form.

At the same time it was a space within which thousands of people from all over London – Caribbean, English and anyone else who cared to turn up – were meeting and mingling, a market-place where everyone was negotiating the construction of a new life. It drew its identity from Caribbean culture, but it wasn't a Caribbean festival, because it was born in London, and at its heart was the experience of being a migrant in Britain. Within the decade in which it established itself, it also presented Londoners with an object lesson in a new kind of relationship with the public spaces of the city.

An obvious comparison was with the military parades which had provided English festivals with a traditional model since Victorian times. Typically, important public events were almost always characterized by their highly controlled and tightly organized form, and their celebration symbolized acceptance of this control. This was a pattern in which highly disciplined participants displayed themselves, in accordance with a strict schedule, to an equally disciplined fringe of delighted spectators, and the entire exercise precisely reflected the hierarchical nature of the country's social organization. In a successful public event nothing unplanned was allowed to take place. Disorder was outlawed or severely restricted to a specific and ritual role – a jester at court, tolerated but insignificant.

The Carnival broke all the rules. In the Carnival the spectators are also the participants. The festival is the festival of anyone who cares to step into the street and take part. There was no symbolic rope separating the subject from the object. The Carnival is for everyone and by everyone. Disorder is its rule; and just as we, the migrants, had been obliged, through the preceding decades, to come to terms with the industrialized patterns of urban life, so London had to begin coming to terms with a model which demanded a symbolic explosion of democracy in its public life.

It was, perhaps, the first time I had a clear understanding that we actually possessed the potential to reshape the city, and this made me determined to stay, even though it was now obvious that I was missing out on the opportunities which had opened up for my relatives in Canada and the USA.

Towards the end of 1973 all my calculations abruptly changed. My father died in New York, and I was just getting over the shock of that event when my long-lost brother turned up. In fact, I'd been hearing news of him for a couple of years, because he was a well-known activist who had been running various campaigns for prisoners' rights and against police harassment. He was also a guru of black 'self-help', and if he had been using the name we called him at home I'd have known immediately who he was. As it was, I telephoned to ask his advice without having any idea of our relationship. During the conversation it turned out that we came from the same country and the same village. Given that we had the same name the odds were that we were related, and in a couple of sentences I knew who he was.

The mood in which I faced my reunion with him was both angry and elated. He had never been far from my thoughts in all these years, first as a puzzle, then as a tragically disappeared, absent hero. Now it was obvious that he had cut himself off from us, apparently without a second thought. He lived in Manchester, but if he had wished to do so he could have located us without too much trouble. The timing of our mutual discovery also had something eerie about it. It must have been pure coincidence, but it was as if he had waited until my father died.

— 5 —

Have a Nice Day

A Story of New York (1976)

My brother-in-law, Gus, had arranged to pick me up at my mother's flat after work, and I was waiting for him with a feeling of pleasant anticipation. This wasn't simply because we were going out for the evening but also because I liked him, probably best of all my friends, and I hadn't seen him to talk with since I had arrived in the country. I had met him, twenty years before, when I was a teenager, and he'd come calling on my sister, back in London. During the next few years I grew to like and respect him. Everyone in the family did. He was reliable and quiet, with an easy temperament. Just the opposite of my sister, who was given to frequent bouts of temper, moody and reputed to be difficult to live with.

My mother and my aunt were already cooking a special meal, one of those home dishes for which they had to do hours of shopping down in Brooklyn, where there were rows of Caribbean shops selling produce flown in daily from Puerto Rico, Jamaica, Trinidad and Guyana. It was typical of Gus to treat my mother's cooking with enthusiasm, even though she was probably the least expert of all the cooks in my family. My eldest sister, for instance, had once lived in France and retained a taste for cooking the fancy food she learned about there. My other two sisters were, by contrast, nationalistic about their cooking, and specialized in versions of the food we'd eaten as children. But many of their friends were from places like Belize, Aruba, Haiti or Puerto Rico, and they cooked the dishes they learned from them, together with the kind of soul food cuisine favoured by our black American cousins.

Most of the family lived within a few miles of each other, and whenever I visited New York I would spend most weekends eating. In any case a visit meant food, and even when I was sitting at home in my mother's flat, it was not unusual for one of the sisters, or a niece or nephew, to turn up with some delicacy which couldn't wait for my arrival. All this was when there was nothing special going on. When there was a party or celebration of any kind, we'd have to be prepared to work our way through some solid feasting.

All this was more or less the way other families we knew lived, but we thought – we, the men, that is – that our family had a special female ambience. Perhaps this was because we were all well aware that the important decisions affecting the family were taken by the women. My father had been the only person who could stand up to them, and until his death he fought them doggedly over issues which were both important and trivial – where they should live, when to move, the paying of bills, the date of my sisters' marriages, what time to eat on Sundays and so on. There was a sense in which his resistance was only symbolic, of course, because it was the women's pioneering spirit which moved us in certain directions. For instance, it had been my mother who had decided they should move to the USA, and had first gone there to live, leaving my father to sell the house in London and follow. It was also the women's urge towards stability that kept a roof over everyone's head in the early days, before my father could find work and earn money.

It took all his strength of will, courage and indomitable stubborness to assert himself as the focal point of the family, and after he died the women took over. That is to say, my mother and three sisters made up a sort of ruling council which took over. By and large, the main decisions affecting the family were now taken by these four. The kitchen was their domain, from which they dispatched messages, condolences, rewards, all in the form of rich, dark pepperpot, curries, pies, black puddings, rice and peas, boned chicken, preserved fruits, fried fish and cakes of every sort.

The only interruption came when there was some sort of important rift or argument between them. Like thunder in Olympus we heard its echoes, and at these times men and children took refuge from bad temper and interminable telephone conversations in my mother's flat, where my aunt, who was always neutral, provided food and calm advice. At times like this we missed our father more than ever. 'There's nobody like the old man,' Gus sometimes said.

My mother married again after my father's death, and somehow the presence of the stepfather made things worse. Not that he was a weakling. On the contrary, he was a tough character; a Garveyite since his youth, he had been a steward on a liner, had sailed the world and been a well-known black man in the city during the worst times for black people. But soon after marrying my mother he had taken a careful account of the situation and now spent most of his time in bed, only emerging to tell stories about the old days, and it was his stated policy never to interfere in family disputes.

Gus had a theory about the family. All the brothers, he said, were sensitive and repressed to the point of being demoralized. It was no accident, he said, that none of us had stable families ourselves, because our female relatives had so spoiled, pampered and bullied us, all at the same time, that it was impossible for us to get on with other women.

'You should all have married each other,' he would sometimes say, and it was difficult to tell whether or not he was joking. In any case, it was true that I loved no woman as much as I loved my sisters. Sometimes we would stay up nearly all night, long after the husbands had given up and gone to bed, talking over old times, telling stories about our father, dancing and singing together in a sort of manic chorus line.

In the middle of this splurge of temperament it was a treat to be with Gus, and to go off for an evening with another man. Even so I was called to the phone at my mother's flat to tell one or other of my sisters the details, like where we intended to go, when we were coming back, and it wasn't until nearly nine, more than two hours after Gus had arrived, that we got away, and started walking down to the subway.

We were going to see Bartley, another boy from home – Gus still called him a boy, as he had during their school-days. Bartley had come over a couple of weeks before and was still illegal, but, as Gus told me, he knew the scene in Brooklyn and he was sure to show us some sport.

On the subway, Gus talked a little about what had been happening. He was a draughtsman working for a construction firm, and work had slackened off during the last two years.

'It's a downward trend,' he said. 'They're laying off people gradually.'

He was management and safe for the moment, which was, we agreed, just as well, because my sister worked for Ma Bell, Bell Telephones, and her salary simply wouldn't be enough to keep them going if there was trouble.

We came up into Brooklyn on a hot, airless night. Once again I experienced that odd feeling of dislocation I felt sometimes when I came across a setting which seemed to belong in a different place. The avenue down which we walked looked like Kingston or Bridgetown or any other Caribbean capital. The same small shops selling Caribbean versions of Chinese and Indian foods, the same small clumps of men scattered on the pavement, playing dominoes or talking, the same snatches of music – heavy on the bass. Over everything was the slow, deep thumping of drums.

'Just like home,' said Gus.

Bartley lived in a street of terraced houses, with stairs running up from the pavement to the front door. He was sitting out on the steps with a couple of men, and he stood up and shook hands as we approached.

'I used to see you and your brother,' he said, 'at music festival.'

He was talking about the annual music festival in Guyana. On these occasions we were dressed in white silk shirts and navy-blue shorts, the uniform of the boys' choir, and we sang a poem by W. H. Davies set to music. I could remember every word of the song, but the sight of Bartley stirred no memories at all. He was now a grown man, over six feet tall, with broad shoulders and a moustache. I couldn't begin to imagine what sort of small boy he had been.

We got into Bartley's car, a battered old Chevy, which lumbered along as if flattening the road beneath it. This was pay-day, one of Bartley's rare nights off, and he was feeling high, pleased and glad of our company. His regular daytime job, in an underground car-park, was badly paid, like any of the jobs which used illegals, but he could just make a living by working long hours. He sent some of his wages back home every week, and once he got his green card his wife and two sons would be joining him.

'That'll be a happy day,' he said.

'What's wrong with the bachelor life?' Gus asked ironically.

'The bachelor life? You're kidding, baby,' Bartley said, breaking into the familiar street black accent. He shouted with laughter, pounding the wheel. 'This town is great if you got money. If not, forget it. Anyhow, when the family's here I'll be saving money.' He gave Gus a sidelong look and grinned. 'I'll be like you then. Money in the bank and food on the table.'

We were rolling slowly past a tiny playground where a number of youths were playing an energetic game of handball. Under the street lights their muscular bodies, bare to the waist, gleamed as they moved from one lightning pose to another.

'The only worry,' Bartley was saying, 'is to make sure she don't get religion. These people only got three vices, man. Drugs, numbers and religion.'

'Those aren't vices,' said Gus,' those are a way of life.'

'The lady in the apartment above me, she's a church sister. She don't play the numbers. All she does is pray and screw. By the time the church finish with her at the weekend she's broke. Ready for another week of misery, Jesus.' Bartley waved his hand. 'Along a street like this you'll have a hundred, if not more. The Church of God. The Church of God in Jesus. The Church of God with Jesus. The Church of God by Jesus. The Church of God for Jesus. The Church of God through Jesus. Ripping off people is the biggest industry in this town, man.'

We turned off the avenue and stopped beside a shop-front. A small sign said 'topless' in red neon. Below this it said 'bar' in blue neon. Bartley pushed open the door and we walked in past a small bar. The room at the back contained about fifteen small round tables with chairs scattered round them and a bank of red plastic seats along one wall. Facing us was a raised platform along the width of the wall at the back, which was one long mirror.

Around us were about a dozen men who, to judge by the way they spoke, were American, not West Indian. Incongruously, it struck me at this point that I hadn't spoken to a white person or even seen one close up since I had arrived. In England that would have been impossible. When I said this to Gus and Bartley they laughed.

'I see enough of them all day, man,' Bartley said. 'Besides, if a white man came down here they'd arrest the sucker for provocation.'

'It's funny to remember that I lived there in England for more than ten years,' Gus said reflectively. 'I can remember everything, the way they talked and the things we used to do, but somehow it didn't make much of an impression on me. I didn't miss it. If I left this country now I'd miss it. I could see myself gradually changing into an American.'

'Your kids are American,' I said. These were my niece and nephew, who had been born in London. In the decade since my parents had arrived here, the rest of the family had become Americans with an ease which, after London, seemed extraordinary. In this city, after the moment when residence became an official fact, there were no tests and no hurdles to climb. To live here was to be American.

'Yes.' Gus paused, thinking about it. 'We're still West Indian inside. But I guess if you look at us from the outside we're an American family.'

'England. The Queen. Tradition.' Bartley uttered the words like a curse. 'Bullshit. I just couldn't deal with all that shit. One thing about this country, you know where you stand. The English are hypocrites. Always were.'

For a moment I felt like arguing with him, pointing out that living in England wasn't like that at all. But in a way he was right, and I didn't have the energy to argue about the sense in which he wasn't.

We ordered beer, which was served by a tall, impassive woman wearing only a short skirt. No one spoke, but Bartley eyed her huge, dark nipples.

'Gimme some,' he muttered as she walked away. He shrugged. 'I might as well look. It's costing me money. Everything in this damn town costs.'

Gus smiled.

'I spent my whole day talking about costs. When it's not costs it's quotas. We're having a big fight over quotas at the moment.' Gus was on a committee which negotiated with the management on behalf of the staff, and a lot of his time was spent on arguments of this kind. 'The Puerto Ricans want to change the basis of the quota. Right now we're in a category with the black Americans. They want to change that, put all the West Indians in together as Caribbeans, and increase that quota. We're fighting that. The way it is we have an advantage over the black Americans because we're usually better qualified. Put us in with the PRs and they'll dominate. Those guys work together and we can't even understand what they're saying.'

'It's happening all over,' Bartley said. 'I've got two of them on the job and you can bet I'm watching my back.'

At that point the lights suddenly went down, leaving only a light above the stage at the end of the room. A woman appeared and began to strip. She was tall, like the waitress, and light-skinned, with curly dark hair which didn't look as if it had been straightened. She writhed and pressed herself against the mirror and took some clothes off.

Around us there were roars of approval. 'Come over here and do that, baby,' one man shouted. 'Where you from?' another bellowed. Near us a man in a straw hat stood up. 'She from Alabama,' he bellowed. 'You from down home, baby?'

The woman continued her dance, smiling obliviously . When she got down to her G-string, the customers began waving dollar bills. 'Here, baby', they shouted from all parts of the room. She came off the stage and began dancing among the tables, sticking out her behind or her crotch, and one man after another draped a note on the G-string. Bartley held up a dollar bill and she came over, wiggling and snapping her hips towards us. Oddly enough, the performance wasn't particularly erotic, because there was something over-whelming and slightly intimidating about her sinuously rolling flesh as she came closer. Bartley gripped her firmly between the legs when she reached our table and poked his dollar into her waistband. That done, she writhed neatly out of his grasp and continued her tour of the room. Soon she was back on the stage. She had got rid of the

G-string and was now lying back, her legs spread wide apart. There was a howl from the audience, and the dollar bills began waving again. But as she started to come off the stage for a second time, there was a commotion at the entrance. Someone shouted in a different tone, a sound which was angry and threatening in comparison with the jovial roars which had greeted the dance.

'Stay where you are,' Gus muttered. He was seated sideways on and could see the entrance. I started twisting round to see what was happening. 'Don't move,' he repeated urgently. 'Just sit quiet.'

In the mirror I could see that some men had come in. One of them seemed to be pointing a shotgun at the room and the others were holding revolvers.

'I can't believe this,' I said.

Suddenly the lights went up, the music stopped and I could see the men clearly. There were three of them, and they were wearing ski masks.

'Up against the wall,' someone shouted. The man with the shotgun waved it at the far wall, and everyone slowly got up and shuffled towards it. One man leaned forward with his hands above his head, palms resting against the wall, and the rest of us followed suit. Somehow my mind couldn't take hold of what was happening, and for a little while I had a vague feeling that in a moment someone would start laughing and we'd find it was all a joke, part of the act.

Behind us one of the men was walking past the line, and as he went he searched through pockets, dropping the money he took into a bag. In my pocket were two twenty-dollar bills my mother had given me before we left the apartment, and now I wished she'd kept them. At the end of the line the masked man got up onto the stage where the dancer was standing, like us, facing the mirror, with her hands resting on it. He riffled through her bag, which lay on the floor at the side of the stage, then he went up behind her and started feeling her nude body. She didn't move, except to hang her head a little while he squeezed her breasts and passed his hands between her legs.

'Come on,' the man with the shotgun shouted. Immediately the other two turned and ran the length of the room and out of the door. The man with the shotgun lingered for a moment, still pointing; then he backed off, turned and vanished. Just before the door slammed he shouted, 'Have a nice day.'

There was a small pause; then everyone began talking at once. It was as if a holiday mood had swept the room, and everyone was caught up in a wave of relief and relaxation. The man in the straw hat began telling Gus that if he had been younger and hadn't a family to think of he would have taken the gun and shoved it up the bandit's ass.

Bartley was the only one who stayed quiet, his face grim and set. Suddenly it struck me that he must have had all his money on him. As an illegal he got paid in cash. I asked him whether he'd lost much.

'Everything,' he said heavily. 'Everything.'

'Let's finish our beer,' I said.

'No way,' he replied. 'I've got to get out of here before the police arrive. One hold-up a night is enough.'

I felt a bit stupid for not thinking of that. I also felt a bit guilty. This had happened because he was showing me around. Most of the club's clientele seemed to feel the same way about the police and we went out in a jostling crowd.

'Don't worry,' Gus told Bartley as we walked to the car. 'Monday, I'll fix you up with something.'

'Thanks,' Bartley said. 'But still.'

He left the sentence unfinished and we got into the car in silence. At the nearest gas station Bartley filled up the Chevy's tank and Gus paid with his credit card. On the way home, as we left Brooklyn and headed towards Queens, Bartley looked back briefly.

'I guess my money will be turning up in the collection on Sunday.'

'No, it won't,' Gus replied. 'It's got to go through a few pushers and numbers men first. It won't turn up in the collection until Sunday after.'

'If only Jesus knew where his bread was coming from,' Bartley said.

When he dropped us off, I still felt bad about Bartley's money. I'd been thinking during the drive about the hours he'd worked to get it, and about his family back home waiting for nothing this week. As I got out, I told him I was sorry. He shrugged.

'That's life in the big city,' he said. 'Two steps forward, one step back.'

Gus's car was parked in front of the apartment, and as we went towards it he put his hand on my shoulder.

'No need to say anything at home about this,' he said. I nodded. He was right. If I told the family what had happened, Gus would be facing reproaches for the next week or more. How could he, they would ask, expose me to a situation of such danger?

We shook hands through the car window. 'At least,' he said, 'you've seen a typical side of the city.'

The apartment was silent, and I tiptoed to my room, got into bed and turned on the small TV set at the foot of the bed. It was an old film with Mae West and Cary Grant, but I couldn't concentrate, and in a short while I turned off the set and settled down to sleep. Just before I drifted off I remembered standing against the wall of the bar with a gun in my back. Images of the St Valentine's Day massacre as I had seen it in several films kept flashing through my mind. Now, a couple of hours later, I felt lucky to be alive. I embraced my pillow with a sudden feeling of delight. Have a nice day, I muttered.

— 6 —

London, 1974 to 1980

I drifted into journalism in the 1970s more or less by default. Working in a school in Paddington, I was interviewed for a documentary about black schoolchildren. Within a couple of weeks the producer had hired me to write and present the show, and during the next year I found myself repeatedly being hired to work on similar projects. The work was easier and more agreeable than anything I had done so far, and before long I was a regular correspondent on an assortment of journals and broadcasting outlets.

As it happened, my new career would have been impossible a few years previously. This was not so much because racial discrimination in the job market had ended. As a freelance I was never to do much more than exist on the fringes of the journalistic world. Instead, it was the breadth and variety of migrant engagement in the life of the city which created new opportunities.

My most lucrative commissions came from the rapidly expanding demand for writing about black music. Over the previous two decades Caribbean migrants in London had created an external market for Jamaican music which had given a crowd of unknown musicians an international stage, but reggae wasn't yet a household word, and most English people had no idea how to pronounce it. One or two Jamaican artists like Desmond Dekker and Jimmy Cliff had penetrated the British charts, but their success had been sporadic, an exotic supplement to a scene dominated by white rock 'n' rollers. The migrant market focused instead on the music sweeping Jamaica. Around West London, throughout the 1960s, a number of tiny record companies, precarious one-man operations on the Kingston model, had specialized in reproducing and marketing authentic Jamaican sounds – ska or R&B, which were often themselves versions of African-American hits. This industry, in its turn, provided a market for its own hardware: hi-fi equipment which could reproduce a thumping bass beat and turntables which allowed discs to be easily and quickly manipulated. In the clubs and parties a new breed of entertainer began to emerge. These were men who had access to collections of new and imported discs, and introduced them with a flow of informative patter.

With the new breed of Rastafarian-inspired reggae musicians, like the Wailers, Toots and Big Youth, the music itself gave the scene a political resonance. The lyrics were riddled with an imagery based on the Rastafarian commentary on life in Jamaica, but it also served to describe black perceptions of our situation in London. For oppression we read harassment and discrimination. For Babylon we read the police. In Africa and the Caribbean the newly independent countries furnished us with a model of cultural autonomy and administrative power, and we knew that in half the world Babylon had been defeated. Everything we heard hinted that the exercise of moral strength and the will to self-determination could deliver freedom from oppression. In the circumstances the response was inevitable, and our language, our style and our social life flowered with a series of coded messages about rebellion and defiance.

At the same time, new alliances were manufacturing themselves around the migrant music and lifestyle. In the previous decade the political left in the city, and its adjuncts in the burgeoning youth culture, had more or less ignored the migrants. The anti-racism which stirred student passions at the time concerned South Africa and the USA. Powellism, however, had given racist politics a new strength in the community. Encouraged and reinforced by the popular support for Powell's hostile speeches, the British National Party, the BNP, complete with distinctive skinhead haircuts and swastika banners, began marching through districts with large migrant minorities, organized new centres and recruited members in football grounds and pop festivals. In response, white liberals had summoned up an active opposition to counter the NF demonstrations. It produced a swathe of white radicals in the cities, whose activism had shifted its focus from the USA or South Africa to their local environments – Handsworth, Brixton or North Kensington – where there were conflicts as spicy as anything to be found abroad. Black music, black slang and black styles began to assume a new interest which increasingly spilled over the borders of the black communities.

London was already reeling from the impact of the industrial conflicts which had taken place in the earlier half of the decade. At the end of 1974 the government, crippled by an overtime ban by the mining and engineering unions, had announced a three-day week for most workers with the aim of cutting electricity consumption by one-fifth. London, in the middle of winter, went through a regular schedule of power cuts and transport stoppages. In the streets there was a distinct feeling that there was no one minding the shop. But this was only a prelude to an era of street battles and demonstrations which reinforced the city's sense of drift and chaos. In West London the anti-racist movement produced its first martyr when the NF organized a demonstration against Asian migrants and, during the fracas, a white anti-racist, Blair Peach, was killed by a blow from a police baton.

By the middle of the decade I had worked on a few TV documentaries about migrants in London, and I was broadcasting for a BBC World Service programme to the Caribbean. Branching out, I took on my first writing commissions as the black music reviewer of a music magazine, *Street Life*. Typically, the editorial board consisted of a mixture of young music journalists and recent graduates steeped in the politics of the student Left. They didn't take much persuading to let me begin writing about the impact of migrant life in London, and within a few years I was writing features and news items for a variety of journals and newspapers in Fleet Street.

I could do this largely because of the role that black people were beginning to assume in the life of the cities. Like most white-collar employers, Fleet Street generally refused to offer black writers staff jobs. At the same time the media couldn't completely ignore migrants because it was clear that in the larger cities, especially

London, we were at the heart of both crisis and change. For example, black people had been confined by discrimination and poverty to some of the worst housing in the city. The solutions involved moving them to vast housing estates dotted around the inner suburbs, and using a new form of organization, housing associations, to pioneer renovation and regeneration in areas like Notting Hill. Similarly, police treatment of black people threw up an endless succession of complaints about wrongful arrests or deaths in custody, and black protests against official indifference and judicial harassment were partly answered by legislation which facilitated the establishment of law and information centres within various communities.

On top of all this, there was a kind of cultural explosion going on among the migrants. The Jamaicans, Trinidadians, Grenadians and Guyanese who had arrived in the previous decade had instantly understood that, over and above their former national status, they now shared a label – West Indians – with everyone else from the Caribbean. In London, events had more gradually converted them into 'blacks'. In addition, most of them had arrived and taken on whatever kind of work they could get, as their compatriots had always done in the Caribbean tradition of seasonal migration. After a decade, however, it was clear that this was a very different enter-prise. They weren't going back, and they had achieved enough security to begin making choices about what they wanted from life. The brightest and most energetic began leaving the sites where they seemed destined to remain on the lowest rung of the ladder. They were largely barred from the managerial and executive jobs they sought, and instead began establishing themselves in whatever fields proved the most congenial. Some started small businesses, travel agencies, import/export, even undertaking. Some found a niche in social work and local government administration. Others took advantage of local government funding to found and staff community and care centres, bookshops, advice and arts centres. They were joined by a generation of their children who were leaving school and coming into a labour market which had already shed most of the jobs their parents had come to do. A substantial minority were headed for inevitable unemployment, but in any case it was preferable, in default of anything better, to join a theatre group or work in a community centre, just to hang out wherever there was the possibility of some action.

The media outlets for which I worked had a vague sense that there were new movements going on 'out there'. Their complement of exclusively white journalists, however, had practically no knowledge or experience of these trends, so, for the time being, there was always work of a kind for someone with my privileged access to the sources. I found myself interviewing writers and musicians and politicians and prisoners, attending performances, arguing with 'experts' on TV and reading the news on local radio.

For a while all this was pure pleasure. Suddenly London had changed its aspect, and this was, I had always supposed, how the other half lived. Now I could walk through police lines merely by flipping a card, without being searched or pushed around. Now stars came tamely to my beckoning microphone, trailing a crowd of nubile attendants who didn't seem to care what end of the business I was in. Now flying into Nairobi, on an all-expenses-paid trip to do research for a TV programme, I found myself marvelling at the fact that only a couple of years before I had been tramping despairingly around Notting Hill wondering how I would raise the money to pay my share of the rent.

From the beginning, it struck me that this was probably an ideal position from which to observe the processes which were beginning to redefine the city's politics and social life, but there was another strong influence at work on me. My older brother lived in Manchester, and he kept urging me to visit him, and to write about black people in the region. As it happened, this coincided with some of my own inclinations. In London I was too often confined to radio and to news items about the latest crisis, but by offering to describe unknown territories of blackness I could persuade editors to let me travel and to write the kind of features I wanted. I was half-serious in any case. There was something about the existence of the black communities in different parts of the country which I found intriguing and exciting. There were few references to them in the media, apart from strongholds of Powellism like Wolverhampton and

Smethwick, where black people seemed to live under constant threat. Why was it, I kept wondering, that they had chosen to live in these places rather than in the relative safety of the capital?

The answer was that each of these communities was rooted in a long and diverse history of settlement, which largely pre-dated the time when I arrived. The odd thing was the extent to which each one had also been shaped by the identity and character of its region. For example, black Liverpudlians dated the time of their presence back to the days of slavery. Since then, the community had been augmented by a steady trickle of West African and Somali seamen. Caribbeans had been relatively recent arrivals, and the core of the community was a large group of mixed-race families who could trace their ancestry back a couple of centuries to an African who had stepped off the boat in Liverpool or moved there from Bristol or Cardiff.

Being in Liverpool at that time felt like being in a different country. The black people I encountered lived in Liverpool 8. Later on, after the riots at the start of the 1980s, the media described the district as Toxteth, but when I first went there everyone called it Liverpool 8. Liverpool 8 was occupied and dominated by black and mixed-race people and the whites who lived with them. If you walked the length of a couple of blocks out of the area in any direction, you were hard put to see anyone who was not white. I met dozens of young people who, during their entire lives, had hardly ventured out of the district marked out by their postcode. To go into the shops in the centre of the city, they said, was to invite arrest, because the local assumption was that if you were black you lived in Liverpool 8, and if you lived there you had to be a thief or a prostitute. In fact, unemployment and poverty were traditional facts of life in the area, and attitudes to the letter of the law were correspondingly lax, but the cordon sanitaire the town had drawn around Liverpool 8 was about race and racist terror of the ethnic brew which characterized the district. It was common, for instance, when I got to know the place, to find myself attending family gatherings presided over by a white grandmother who spoke with the accent of Cork or Dublin, while the black grandfather alternated between uncertain English and some West African language. Around them would be a host of relatives whose skin sported every shade from Celtic pallor to African aubergine.

In Manchester the mixture was a little different. Moss Side was Manchester's equivalent of Toxteth, and though a large slice of the community consisted of mixed-race families who had moved down from Liverpool, the tone was set by West Indians who had been servicemen during the war and remained there, or had come back to the town soon after. Their isolation was just as intense. Like Toxteth, Moss Side was black, packed with crumbling multi-occupied terraces and riddled with shebeens, gambling and drinking dens, and clubs. Within half a mile outside of Moss Side, however, it was rare to see a black or brown face. This was a familiar pattern during the 1970s when I travelled around the North, the Midlands and the West Country. In Bristol, black people were corralled in St Paul's. In Cardiff, Tiger Bay. In Birmingham, Handsworth. Within these enclaves they seemed to speak and behave in a style that, to a stranger, was indistinguishable from that of their white neighbours. In comparison, we had been able to open London's structures and impose our presence in a way that seemed unimaginable in Leeds or Nottingham or Wolverhampton. Yet even while I was making this comforting observation, the geography of the black communities around the country seemed to hint at the disturbing notion that, like the black Liverpudlians, we had all been isolated from the outside world, stripped of our legitimate heritage and firmly ghettoized. It was an idea partly provoked by the ferment of the 1970s. In London we had mingled the internationalizing idiom of blackness with the universal rhetoric of liberation in order to validate our claims to our new territory. At the same time the identity we were defending had become as much to do with London itself as with our origins.

Basil and Stuart's ball

(from the *New Statesman*, May 1980)
Britain's ethnic newspapers over the last few weeks have been carrying a number of full page adverts for a 'Spring Ball', which was held last week at the Grosvenor Hotel. It was a typically

Tory event (carriages at 2 pm), but the participants were mainly West Indian. The whole affair was part of the continuing Conservative attempts to woo the immigrant, which have gone unnoticed by most people, both black and white. This is because the thrust of Tory self-advertisement, in the case of the West Indian community, is carried by two Jamaican businessmen, Basil Lewis, a Haringey travel agent and councillor, and Stuart Weathers, owner of the Clapham plumbing firm 'Help'.

The dynamic duo are notorious for vying with each other for Conservative favours, and as the immigrant vote emerges in certain marginal constituencies as more and more important, they find themselves in greater demand at Central Office. So far Lewis has been thought to be ahead in the race for Tory esteem. He is a fervent admirer of Margaret Thatcher, and during the last election in Haringey, to the embarrassment of the Tory candidate who was trying to play down such issues in front of immigrant voters, he was loud in his support of law and order policies. He is, however, a small quiet man, eager to organise community events.

Weathers, on the other hand, is a flamboyant character, whose claims are as dashing as his suits. Some time ago he was said to be feeling disillusioned after failing to be elected to the executive of the local party, and he caused the Tories some embarrassment by kicking up a fuss when he was ushered to what he said was an obscure table at a Conservative function. He is also ostentatiously proud of his contacts with leading Conservatives, and pictures of himself with Heath and Thatcher adorn his office wall.

But there was no sign of coolness last week at the ball. A large proportion of the West Indian business community turned out to see the fun. They were treated to a fashion display; they were awarded prizes provided by Caribbean Airways and by that sturdy arm of reactionary Jamaican business interests, *The Gleaner*; and they were entertained by the spectacle of plumber Weathers wandering about with a large snake draped about his neck.

The minister's speech was the expected exhortation. He said that the onus was on blacks to make their requirements known to the government, and this could only be done by taking part in politics. The crowd of potential Conservative politicians took this less enthusiastically than might have been expected. As law-abiding, middle-aged, anti-welfare state business persons, they found it hard to understand why the Tories hadn't sent along a spokesman from Trade and Industry, or an expert on small businesses, or even a tame peer to lend the event some social cachet. What they got was Patrick Jenkin, Secretary of State *for the Social Services*, and as if to ram the point home he was accompanied by John Wheeler, chairman of the Commons sub-committee, which reported recently on the suss laws and black youth. As one businessman commented after listening to Patrick Jenkin: 'Perhaps they're trying to tell us something.'

Stuart Weathers, incidentally, was in the habit of taking his pet snake draped round his neck to Conservative occasions, and he once held it out to Mrs Thatcher and asked her to stroke it. There is no record of her reply.

— 7 —

The Smell of the Coast

An African Story (1974)

Part 1

I met Hadida at the beginning of my second day on the coast. I had come directly from Nairobi, and I was feeling tired and disorientated. The trip had started in disappointment. The truth was that it was hard to believe I was in Africa, just as many years later, looking back, it was hard to believe I had ever been there. From the time I got off the plane I was constantly assailed by images which were strange yet familiar, as if reality was somehow slipping beneath my gaze. At some point in the afternoon I had sat on the large, shadowy verandah of a hotel drinking beer. From the ceiling was suspended a large, creaking, metal fan, which reminded me immediately of public buildings in the town where I was born: the library, the courthouse. Around me, Africans dressed in short-sleeved shirts, ties and sandals spoke in rapid Swahili, but I found myself continually straining to listen, as if by that effort I would be able to understand. After all, if I half-closed my eyes it would be easy to imagine that I was back home where I had grown up.

Later on I left my bags at the hotel, and went to the nearby post office to cable back to the producer of the programme for which I was working that I had arrived, and would shortly be on my way to meet the man we were to interview. When I had finished, I sat on the wall outside looking at the scene in the street. The action was in itself reassuring. Since arriving in England I hadn't been in a country where almost everyone was black. Looking down the street in every direction I could only see black faces. Gazing at this scene gave me a chance to examine how I felt. There was more. During my boyhood

I had spent a great deal of my spare time leaning on a fence, or sitting on a wall in the sunshine talking to my friends, looking at the passers-by. This had been a part of how I had lived, and suddenly it was as if that memory had emerged from a long oblivion.

I had only been there a few minutes when an old man wearing denim shorts and a striped sweater came up and spoke to me in Swahili. I shrugged. 'I don't understand,' I said. The old man stared. 'I don't speak Swahili,' I said. 'I come from abroad. Outside of Africa.'

The old man was silent for a moment.

'Where are you from?'

I told him.

'England?' He looked annoyed, as if I were teasing him. 'You are not an Englishman. Where do you come from?'

'The Caribbean,' I replied, uncertain that he would recognize the name of my own country. He frowned and glared at me in puzzlement.

'Are you a negro?'

'I am an African,' I said.

'No. You are not,' he replied fiercely. A little daunted, I began to explain that the black people in my country were descended from Africans. He interrupted irritably.

'Where is it?'

I cast around for a country he would have heard of. 'South America.'

He caught at the word. 'America. America,' he repeated triumphantly. 'You are negroes there.'

Giving up, I moved away. As I went, I could feel him staring after me, a sneer on his face.

Later in the afternoon, just as the sun was beginning to go down, I caught the coast bus to Mombasa. It was a rickety old bus with seats made of wooden slats and window frames with no glass in them. By the time we moved off it was crowded. Most of my fellow passengers seemed to be traders of some sort, to judge by their luggage. There were suitcases packed to bursting with fabrics or groceries of various kinds. Some people carried fat bundles on their heads, others had baskets full of squawking poultry. I had travelled on buses like this before. A vagrant memory kept occurring to me. It was about a trip I had made with my mother just before Christmas when we had taken a bus like this from our village into the middle of town. We had spent a long time looking at the shop-windows, and when we got back to the bus I was tired. On a neighbouring seat there was another little boy and his mother, and this boy kept taking out his willy and pulling at it. His mother kept on smacking his hand and making him put it back, but after a few minutes out would come the willy again. 'Why is he doing that?' I asked my mother again and again, but she, choking with amusement, turned my head towards the window and talked to me about parts of the town we were passing through.

Now, looking out of the window into the Kenyan night, all I could think about was my mother. She wouldn't know I was in Kenya. Indeed, I didn't know myself what country she was in. Wondering about that fact I slid into sleep.

I woke to the sound of singing. Just outside the window a small boy was shouting rhythmically and repeatedly, 'Mayai. Chemsha mayai.'

He held up a tray of boiled eggs. We had pulled into a huge square ringed by shops and stalls. Getting off the bus I felt a sort of disturbance at the fact that I recognized the scene. It was almost identical to the market square in my home village. A sort of courtyard ringed by small groups of lounging men. As I walked across it, a legless beggar blocked my path, cupped hand outstretched. The shop I entered was a small box with barely enough room for three people. It sold everything, broken down into the smallest possible units: half-ounces of butter wrapped in a fold of sugar paper, a handful of tiny peppers, a pint of kerosene. I bought a bottle of mineral water, with a rusty cap. It was warm and tasted of nothing very much, but I gulped it down gratefully, just in time to get back onto the bus. It was hard to fall asleep again. Now that we had left the town far behind, the night pressed down like a rich, deep-pile carpet which seemed close enough to touch. From time to time a winking light gleamed faintly through the dark and the bus slowed down, eventually shuddering to a stop in front of someone carrying a basket of fruit or a clump of agitated chickens. Stops like these only took a couple of minutes, and I had nearly drifted off to sleep when the bus pulled up in front of a sort of open-air café. This, the fat woman next to me said, was the half-way point between Nairobi and the coast. All the passengers got out and sat at the tables dotted around the yard. After the clattering roar of the engines the drowsy passengers seemed reanimated. They talked and laughed as if it was a picnic. Noticing me sitting by myself, two girls strolled over and spoke to me in Swahili.

This happened again and again. Women seemed to have no inhibitions about speaking to a man, especially one on his own, and all through the trip I was mildly surprised to find women approaching me and starting a conversation in a way I had never experienced in Britain.

I told them I didn't speak Swahili and then had to go through the explanation about what I was doing there, why I couldn't speak an African language and so on. But these young women were interested and sympathetic, unlike the old man. I began to enjoy myself. Sitting there in the middle of the night I felt relaxed, and for the first time I was at home, one of the crowd.

When we moved off again it was long after midnight. The passengers, settling in after the break, were still chatting noisily. Suddenly the bus was flooded with the scent of flowers, as strong as if a bunch of exotic sprays had been thrust under my nose. Startled, I asked my neighbour, the fat woman whose bottom had been cushioning me all the way from Nairobi, what the smell was. That was the smell of the coast, she said.

'The coast,' I repeated.

'Yes,' she said with a touch of impatience. 'The flowers of the coast.'

It was hard to believe. The coast must have been fifty miles away, but all through the rest of the journey I was bathed in the scent of flowers growing stronger and stronger like a current going directly to the brain.

When I woke up again the sky was turning grey. The stars had disappeared and we were passing through a town. Mombasa, my neighbour said urgently. Mombasa. But she hadn't needed to tell me, because I recognized the place from the two huge elephant tusks arching across the road. I had seen innumerable postcards with pictures of these tusks. Summoning up my numbed reflexes I stumbled off the bus, dragging my bag behind me.

It was early, about five, and there was no one else in the street. All the shops were closed. My first contact with the Ministry of Tourism would be unavailable, I had determined, until half-past eight. For the moment all I could do was to stand beside the road trying to decide which way to go.

I looked around. On the horizon there was a pale gleam of yellow and red. Above me towered trees I vaguely recognized. Perhaps they were mangoes. At that moment I heard the bristling, whirring sound of wings in the trees. Looking up I saw the flash of one, then two, then a huge crowd of birds, scattering noisily out of the trees into the sky. At first in the morning light they looked grey, then I realized they were green. Parrots. Simultaneously I felt tears springing, unforced, to my eyes. For a moment I was bewildered by the emotion, then just as suddenly I remembered the parrots.

Every morning until I left the village where I was born, I had listened to the same sound, parrots flying out of the mango trees where they nested overnight. Unconsciously I was listening for a series of cock-crows, the other familiar morning sound which had been part of my daily life. Listening, I stood by the roadside, struggling with the sense that all this was unreal, a fantasy of the mind.

After a while I noticed a neon sign some distance away. It seemed to be a bar, and I could hear faint strains of music. I walked slowly towards it, wondering whether by this hour of the morning they'd be willing to serve me coffee. As I grew closer some women emerged from the bar and climbed into a waiting taxi, which drove down the road past me. But after travelling a few yards it stopped and reversed rapidly, pulling up beside me. The woman in the front passenger seat leaned out.

'Hey, pretty boy,' she said, 'pretty boy. Come here.'

I went, and inevitably she asked me what I was doing there, first in Swahili, then in English when I said I didn't understand. Her English had a lilting inflection, but it was more fluent than that of anyone I had run into so far. I explained that I had come to interview a man who lived on the coast for a TV programme in England. Everyone listened impassively, and when I had finished, the women in the front turned round and rapidly translated for her two friends in the back. They all giggled and the taxi driver said something I couldn't catch.

'Are you telling me the truth, pretty boy?' the girl said, turning back to me.

'Yes,' I replied. 'Why would I lie to you?'

'I don't know,' she said thoughtfully, 'but it's not every day we find a boy like you standing by the road.'

At this point one of the girls in the back said something impatiently while staring at me.

'Okay,' my friend in the front seat said. 'Come with me. Get in. Get in,' she repeated. 'You can come home with me.' She paused and grinned mischievously. 'You're not frightened of me?'

I started to climb into the back seat, but the woman sitting nearest to me didn't move.

'Sit in the middle,' said my friend.

I squirmed over into the middle of the back seat, and the taxi moved off before I was settled so that I fell over my travelling companions. Everyone laughed. Now I was cramped into the dark intimacy of the taxi I was disturbingly conscious of their soft, smooth skin and the perfumed warmth of their bodies. My friend in the front seat was looking back at me ironically but when she spoke it was in Swahili to her friends. They all laughed again.

'What's your name?' I asked.

'Honey,' she said. I told her mine and we introduced ourselves all round. But it didn't lead on to more general conversation as I'd hoped, because the driver said something and they all began to talk at once. In a moment I realized that each of the women on either side of me was stroking one of my thighs. I looked at them out of the corner of my eyes, but both were chattering away seriously and not looking at me. To object would have been slightly ridiculous, I thought; besides, I was enjoying it, so I relaxed into the seat, almost drifting into sleep again as we drove along.

After a few minutes the taxi stopped, and Honey opened the front door and got out. I scrambled after her.

'Give the driver some money,' she said. I showed her the small change I had in my pocket. She took some of it out of my hand and gave it to him. 'That's enough,' she said.

As the taxi drove off the girls in the back seat waved mockingly, but Honey had already turned away and was leading me into her yard. As I'd half expected it was familiar like the shops, the trees, the parrots. The house, a long, low structure built on short piles, was arranged on three sides of a courtyard. In one corner there was a communal bath and toilets. A railed verandah ran the length of the yard. Honey's room was larger and better furnished than I'd expected, though. There was a double bed in one corner by the latticed wall. In the middle of the room was a small settee and armchair, all in light, curving wood, like a set of Habitat furniture, and in another corner was an alcove with a little stove in it. She offered me tea. I accepted, and she went to make it, talking all the time as she bustled around the room. She wasn't out so late very often, but last night had been a friend's birthday. The town was deserted at this time of year and she wanted to go to Nairobi. She wanted to go abroad as well. To Europe where there was so much money and so many different people. How much had I paid for my jeans? She was seventeen years old, she told me, a fact I found hard to believe in view of her manner when we had met. She didn't treat me as if she was five years younger, but she did look like a 17-year-old, with a slender, well-shaped body and a cheeky urchin's face. She was also a Muslim, born on the coast, not far from Mombasa. Honey was not her real name, she told me when I asked. Her real name was Hadida, the name of the Prophet's second wife, but foreigners found it difficult to say, so she called herself Honey. A German tourist had given her that name. He was very nice, a great friend, and one day she might go to Germany to see him.

She showed me a picture of the German, a red-faced youth grinning under his blond moustache and holding up a glass of beer to the camera. There were other relics of the German: a postcard, a charm bracelet and a book of Scandinavian pornographic photos.

In that setting the expanses of pink flesh and straw-coloured hair looked weird, grotesque. Honey watched me knowingly. 'Men like those,' she said.

Soon after, she went out for a bath. I lay back in the armchair, dreaming, listening to the sound of water splashing. She would, I knew, be scooping water out of a bucket with a tin can, perhaps an old coffee can, and pouring it over herself. In my childhood we had bathed in this way. Every morning about five, we had woken up to the sound of my uncle at the stand-pipe in the yard, pouring water over himself.

The memory wove in and out of my consciousness, giving everything an odd, blurred quality. When Hadida came back I realized that I must have been half-asleep, because I woke up. In one corner of the room the sun was making little square patterns through the latticed wall. From somewhere outside there was the faint sound of voices. Wrapped in a huge white towel, her hair glistening with drops of water, Hadida looked slender, innocent, exotic. But I knew by now that she was a prostitute. She spent her nights in bars, and slept, I thought, with a random selection of tourists, like the grinning German whose photo she'd shown me. The idea alarmed and revolted me. She could have any kind of disease.

'Let's go to bed,' she said.

She threw the towel onto a chair and walked towards the bed. As graceful as a gazelle. I had never seen a gazelle but the image came unforced. She belonged, I thought, in the *Arabian Nights*.

'I'll stay here,' I said. I was trying not to sound as uncertain as I felt, but her smile as she looked at me grew ironic.

'No,' she said, 'you can sleep with me. It's better. Come on.'

The thought of being outfaced by this kid changed my mood. After all, I had no need to worry about what would happen next or about being found out. I was away from all of that, with no reason to feel apprehensive or guilty. I got up, went over to the bed and lay down beside Hadida. Almost immediately I sat up again, because I'd found myself lying on what felt like soft crumbs. I picked one off my arm where it was clinging, and looked at it. The crumb was the petal of a flower. The bed was covered with them, and whenever we moved we crushed a petal, which gave off an intoxicating whiff of scent.

'You want to make love?' Hadida asked.

For a moment I couldn't reply. Less than an hour before I had been standing by the side of the road wondering what to do. Now I was lying in a bed strewn with rose petals, with this creature from the *Arabian Nights*. The thought occurred to me that I was being gullible. It was all too easy, such things didn't happen.

'What will all this cost me?' I asked, keeping my voice carefully casual to disguise my embarrassment and nervousness. But she sat up abruptly and jerked away from me.

'Cost? What cost?' she said angrily. She paused, and then went on in a calmer tone. 'If you came up to me in a bar and said that I wouldn't speak to you.'

Her indignation embarrassed me again. She was only being kind, I thought, and I felt guilty now for looking at her as a European would have done.

In a moment, however, she smiled, and propping herself up on her elbow began to stroke my penis gently. In my turn I reached between her legs and she spread her thighs a little to make it easier. For a moment we lay there silently touching each other. She was smooth and hairless, with only a tiny patch of soft fuzz above the parting. After a while she leaned over and tried to kiss me but I turned my head away. I felt more or less incapable of making any move towards her or of responding to anything she did. The picture of the women emerging from the club, the taxi-driver's sly, gold-toothed smile, the grinning German, all kept recurring in my mind. Suddenly Hadida got up and knelt astride me. She reached down, and taking my penis in her hand again, began to rub it slowly against herself. At this point my sense of danger reasserted itself. I could catch anything, I thought.

'Have you got anything I could put on?'

She stared at me, puzzled. 'You know,' I mimed the action. I couldn't think of a word that might be familiar to her. She chuckled, the ironic expression back on her face.

'Don't be afraid,' she said. 'I'm not sick.'

I smiled my assent, but in that instant I realized that my penis, which had been more or less erect, was now limp. I strained at it mentally, willing it back to its former stiffness, but it remained slack in Hadida's hand.

She tried for a while, stroking it, then caressing my body and going back to rub my obdurately flaccid penis. Nothing did any good, and eventually she gave up. I could think of nothing to say, and we lay, without speaking, on the flower-scented bed, until I realized she had dozed off. I got up then and dressed myself. She woke up as I was about to go out of the door, and I told her I would come back to see her. She nodded tiredly, and I went out into the sunshine which was already blazing down on to the dusty street.

In a couple of hours I had made contact with the man I was to interview, and he invited me to stay with him a few miles outside Mombasa. On the second day I returned to the town to meet our cameraman, and checked into one of the local hotels.

That night after dinner on the long verandah, I strolled down to the club where I had first seen Hadida. She wasn't there and I didn't recognize any of the other girls. It was a small, rather dingy place, with a jukebox and a bar, from behind which a beaming barman dispensed drinks to a crowd of tourists, mainly German, and an equal number of locals. In the dark the women went from table to table, strutting extravagantly, posing with the Germans, laughing outrageously at everything that was said. I noticed one girl who stopped by a table near mine and sat in the lap of one of the tourists seated there. He winked at his friends and they clinked glasses together, but after a short while the girl got up and walked over to me, grinning broadly. She had the tall, slender body I associated with Somalis, and when she got to me she leaned on the table and said something in Swahili. I told her I didn't understand.

'What?' she said. 'A black man like you? You don't speak Swahili?'

I explained. I asked her about herself and she told me she was Somali. Suddenly she sat down.

'You like me?'

I told her I did.

'But not love?'

She pronounced love with a long vowel, making it sound erotic. I shook my head.

'Not tonight.'

She stared at me for a moment, then shrugged, got up and went back to the Germans. A little depressed by the incident I went back to my hotel. Sometime during the night I decided to go and see Hadida the following day. I found her house in the afternoon. She had just got up, and she sat curled up in an armchair painting her toenails.

I was pleased to see her. She was, in a manner of speaking, my only friend in the country, and I told her what I had been doing. The producer, Tony, was due to arrive in the morning, and I told her about him. She listened solemnly without expression, but when I mentioned his arrival she looked interested.

'He's your friend?'

I said yes, and went on to explain to her what he did.

'I'll bring him to meet you,' I said. 'Maybe you can show us around?'

She made a face.

'He won't want to meet girls,' she said.

'No,' I protested. 'He will. He'll certainly want to meet you.'

'No,' she said firmly. 'He's your friend.'

She must have seen my puzzlement because she put down her nail polish and pointed at me.

'You are homosexual. He's your friend. When he comes no girls.'

I was too taken aback to be fully coherent. I began stammering out my explanations for what had happened that morning. I was tired. She was a strange person. The circumstances were extraordinary. The more I talked, the more her face set in an expression which was kindly but determinedly sceptical, and even when I tried to explain, I understood that she'd found my manners strange and outlandish in the first place. My behaviour in her bed that night had explained my peculiarity. When I talked about the friend who was joining me she became sure. There was no shifting her, unless I could have upended her on the spot and proved my manhood by screwing her vigorously. I considered it for a moment, but only a moment. Anything I did might simply compound the misunderstanding. She had resumed painting her toenails. All I could do was get up and go.

At the door I looked back, intending to say I would come back and see her, but I changed my mind. There was no point. She had ceased to be interested in me long ago and we would only bore each other. She waved goodbye, her manner kindly but indifferent, and as I pulled the door shut behind me I had the feeling she'd already forgotten I had been there.

Part 2

On the night I'm thinking of, I had dinner with an army lieutenant, the director of the local tourist bureau, who was also chairman of the junior chamber of commerce, and the head of the local branch of an import–export firm.

We dined by candlelight on the terrace of the local hotel just outside Mombasa. I had come back for a couple of days because our cameraman had been obliged to return to Nairobi, and we were having a brief holiday. The director had gone somewhere up the coast but I had returned to Mombasa to see Estelle, who ran the import–export business. I had met her the previous week with Mimi, who worked for the tourist bureau and had been helping us to set up locations. We had taken to each other right away, and arranged to meet when I came back to Mombasa. She had brought along Mimi and James, the army lieutenant. It was a good idea because we were all about the same age, and it was pleasant to be one of the party, sitting on the wide marble terrace under the stars.

There was a lot to talk about. Both James and Mimi had studied in Britain, and they talked about what they remembered of it with affection and with a certain cynicism that amused and interested me. Curiously they talked about Britain in much the same way as they talked about any of the other European countries – France, Germany, Switzerland – they had visited. None of them seemed to regard Britain as the unavoidable metropolis. Mimi, who originally came from Madagascar, and spoke French with as much facility as she did English, talked about Switzerland, which had made an extraordinary impact on her. James had found himself living in Aberystwyth, a place whose very name he pronounced with a sort of incredulous delight. For them, normality was this town, its population a hotch-potch of Muslims, Christians, inland tribes, Indians, Europeans, Africanized Arabs and Arabized Africans, rubbing shoulders with people from up and down the coast, from South Africa to Ethiopia. All this they found commonplace.

Estelle was the only one who had not been abroad to Europe. The odd thing was that she reminded me of a girl from my village half-way across the world, and the more I got to know her the more I felt I understood and liked her. She came from a village up the coast and belonged to a minor tribe, one of those whose members were mere peasants, villagers. Their number was small, and they had no links with prominent businessmen or politicians. As such they had no relationship or favour with stronger and more influential groups like the Kikuyu or the Luo. Estelle had been sent to the town early when she was about eleven years old to live in the house of a distant relative and go to school. After she left school and went to work she became her family's sole wage earner, and now four younger brothers and sisters had left the village to live with her, all going to school and starting work on their own account.

'I'd like to go,' she said. 'Maybe in a couple of years I'll come to see you in London?'

'It's a dull place,' I said.

That morning Estelle had taken me to see the Arab dhows coming into harbour, their sails dipping into sight from a long way across the Indian Ocean. The ritual journey had an awesome antiquity – magical, like a fairy-tale come to life. If Aladdin had come down the gangplank this morning and offered to sell me a lamp I'd have bought it, I told them. 'This is the most exciting place I've ever been in.'

Everyone laughed.

'I would like to see somewhere different,' Estelle said. She laughed again and put her hand on my arm. 'I want to see how you live in London.'

Everyone laughed again. In that setting the whole idea seemed ludicrous. It was even more so out in the country, I told them, where the size of the landscape made me feel cut off and separated from everything familiar. I had never stayed in a spot so isolated as the place where we were filming – a group of buildings on the shores of a lake, surrounded by huge, empty countryside. At night on the neighbouring hills, we could see lights and hear the music of drums. There were small villages on that hill, we were told, and a couple of nights previously I had set out to walk to one of them. At first the road was wide and easy, then it began to climb and narrowed to a track, and suddenly I found myself in the middle of a forest of small trees and tall grasses, which obscured the moonlight. At that moment I realized I didn't know where I was going or what lay around the next bend. I could see no lights. Indeed I could hardly see the track in front of me, and the sound of the drums was now muffled and hollowed, sinister. Quickly, I turned and hurried back the way I had come. On the way I remembered a couple of things which hadn't seemed important to me until then. For example, the compound where we stayed was guarded all night by a small patrol of men with large sticks and flashlights, and after dark the gate was locked. Eerily, I saw no one at all during my walk, but I reached the locked gate with an intense feeling of relief. I hadn't mentioned this to anyone else, because, in the daylight, looking across the smiling countryside, the terror I had experienced seemed inappropriate and slightly ridicu-lous. But when I told my friends at the table how I had got lost, their reaction surprised me. All three of them looked serious, and for a moment there was a pause in the conversation.

'Never do that again,' Estelle said. 'If you want to go somewhere at night in this place, take a taxi. It's very dangerous.'

Across the table James nodded seriously. 'You must be careful,' he said.

'What would happen?' I asked.

'Nothing,' Mimi said smoothly. 'Probably nothing. But it's foolish to go around in these lonely places at night.'

For a moment there was an awkward feeling around the table, which Estelle dispelled by telling us about an incident which had happened to her a few days before. She always had her eyes open for a bargain, because, as she explained for my benefit, foodstuffs – rice, beans, oil – were usually in short supply, and it was important to stock up when they arrived in the town. So whenever she saw a queue, on her way to work, during the lunch-hour or on her way home, she would join it, emerging with whatever was on offer. On this occasion she had seen the queue during her lunch-hour, and had found herself standing behind the messenger boy from her office. The messenger boy, actually a middle-aged man, was unaware of her presence as he stood laughing and joking with his friends, and it was some time before she could attract his attention. But when she did so he looked startled and embarrassed to see her. 'What are you doing here?' he asked.

'The same as you,' Estelle replied. 'What are they selling? Is it rice?'

Rice had been expected for some time. But instead of answering the man began to laugh uncontrollably.

'Why are you laughing?' Estelle asked, a little piqued by his behaviour.

'I'm sorry,' he said. 'It's just that this is a line for a woman.'

At that point she realized that everyone in the queue was male.

'That is what they do in their lunch-hour, these men,' she said.

Afterwards Estelle drove me back to my hotel. It was late, and she could only stay for a couple of hours because she didn't want to leave her brothers and sisters alone. In the dark she told me more about herself. She was ambitious. She had got her present position in the firm after starting as a secretary, but now she was unlikely to get any further without proper qualifications. She had to spend some time in Europe, she said. In her line of work no one would take her seriously otherwise.

I walked down the stairs to say goodbye. The hotel was built in a sort of L-shape around an inner courtyard and my room was reached by an outside staircase. But as we walked past the lobby we heard a muffled scream and raised voices.

Looking for the night clerk, we went into the lobby, but there was no one at the desk. After a moment, however, we heard footsteps on the stairs and the man came walking down.

'What's the matter?' I asked him.

He shrugged sullenly. 'I don't know,' he muttered. 'A crazy girl.'

By this time a girl had appeared behind him on the stairs. She was tall, Asian, young, about eighteen years old perhaps.

'What's the matter?' I asked her, as the clerk walked around me and went back to his desk.

'He was attacking me,' she said.

The man laughed sarcastically. He glanced at Estelle and moved to the other side of the desk, pulling me with him, so that she couldn't hear what he was saying.

'She wouldn't pay, this crazy girl,' he said. 'She said she had no money and I told her she could stay in one of the empty rooms. I just went to make sure she got out early in the morning, and then she started acting crazy.'

'Come on,' I said. 'You must have done something.'

'They're crazy, these people,' he replied. 'I was doing her a favour.'

All this time the girl was talking rapidly and energetically to Estelle, who caught my eye at that point and nodded to me. When I went over, she said she would take the girl home with her for the night.

'Are you sure?' I asked her. She was composed and businesslike, as if this was merely another trivial incident in the day, to be dealt with as a matter of course.

'Thank you,' the Indian girl said effusively. 'I don't know what I would have done if you hadn't come.'

Nodding and smiling faintly, Estelle ushered her out to the car which stood in the driveway, and when she was seated in it, closed the door on the flood of speech which had continued from the moment we arrived.

'Is it all right?' I asked Estelle. 'Are you doing the right thing?'

'I think so,' she said. 'I don't know how or what was happening, but it will be no trouble to keep her for the night.'

After they'd driven away I began walking back, thinking about this new side of Estelle. Her decisiveness had surprised me. As I went past the lobby I heard the desk clerk calling me.

'What is it?' I asked him.

'There's an extra charge,' he said.

'An extra charge?' I was bewildered for a moment.

'You had the woman in your room tonight,' he said. He didn't look at me but his tone was full of spite.

Back in my room, before falling asleep, I thought briefly about the man's reaction to our intervention. There had been something confidential, conspiratorial about the way he'd told me the girl was crazy. Perhaps he had expected me to side with him. Perhaps because she was an Asian, perhaps because she was a woman. Perhaps he had spoken to me as he would have to another Kikuyu. It was hard to tell, but I suspected his anger was also a kind of disappointment in my response. I'd been in the country long enough to know that many of the people whom we met saw the Asians as a hostile exploitative tribe. Apart from the Sikh film crew, I hadn't met any, but most of the shops I'd seen were run by Indians. Stepping into one of these large, cool emporia was like going back to my childhood. This was an indelible memory, the tall bolts of cloth from behind which would appear women in saris and spectacles wielding tape-measures, or a pair of tall brothers deep in conversation. In shops like these my mother and grandmother had strolled and talked and haggled for hours, while I loitered gazing at the Aladdin's cave of goods, or searching among the inevitable clutch of children at the back for a schoolfriend.

Sometimes, in Nairobi, I would see the familiar shopkeepers standing or sitting on the pavements in the shade of the awnings – people of business and gold-rimmed spectacles – and sometimes two or three Indian youths would racket past in an open sports car, laughing and shouting to each other, seeming as different from their sober elders as chalk from cheese. Around them the African faces grew closed and impassive. All this I recognized. Perhaps, I thought, if I'd been part of the country I wouldn't have been so quick to interfere.

The following day the manager greeted me on the terrace in his usual friendly fashion.

'I had some trouble with your man last night,' I told him.

I told him about the incident, and when I got to the part about the extra charge he laughed. 'That doesn't apply,' he said. 'I'll speak to him.'

He changed the subject then, without asking for more details or expressing any curiosity about the girl and her situation. For a moment I was about to press him; then it struck me that both he and the clerk were Kikuyu, maybe relatives, and I changed my mind.

Later on Estelle was calm and neutral about what had happened. The girl told her that she came from a prosperous family in Nairobi, her brother was a police inspector and her parents ran their own business. But since she left school a short while before, she had been travelling around the country on a shoe-string budget, staying where she could and moving about by bus or hitch-hiking. The night before, she had said, the clerk had told her she could stay in an empty room, then he had come up and tried to rape her.

'I thought that was it,' I said.

Estelle said nothing for a moment. She looked thoughtful.

'There's something funny about her,' she said eventually. 'Families like that don't usually let their daughters travel around the country alone. I couldn't work it out, and I don't think he would have taken the risk of letting her stay in the hotel unless she'd promised him something.'

'You think she's lying.'

'I don't know,' Estelle said. 'But there was more to it than she told me.'

That was all she would say on the subject. I wished then I had been able to talk to the girl myself, but now there was no more to be said or discovered about the event.

On the terrace Estelle looked at me and smiled ironically.

'It's not like England here,' she said.

Before I could reply, the manager joined us. They were fellow members of the Chamber of Commerce and knew each other well, and they began talking about the meeting that would take place the following week. Around us, the hotel guests, a mixture of European tourists and Africans, chatted quietly. Glasses and coffee cups clinked. Had I not been able to see the desk clerk going about his business in the distance it would have been a cheerful, reassuring scene.

— 8 —

Two Stories of the Caribbean (1977–8)

Jean and Dinah

I had never stayed in such a luxurious hotel before. The reception was a huge barn of a place, timbered in the traditional Caribbean style with slates on top. This led out on to a terrace, where the guests ate their meals. The terrace looked out on to the sea. When the tide came in the waves came to within a few inches of the terrace's edge. From the reception area you walked out into a space, facing the sea. To the left was a large open-air kitchen where men in white coats and chef's hats busied themselves preparing the food; to the right, at a distance of about the length of a cricket pitch, was a bar. Along the beach stood some short palms, but they weren't the sort of coconut trees I remembered from my youth in the Caribbean. These were late-comers, planted after the native coconut trees had withered and died from a species of blight.

This terrace was the heart of the hotel. Around it, in a scattered crescent, stood a number of beach cottages. These were not the sort of beach cottage a beachcomber might live in, with odd bits of wood hammered together and coconut leaves thatching the roof. No such thing. These were small and luxuriously appointed houses. Upstairs in the bedroom there was a four-poster bed large enough for four people. Around the outside ran a balcony. On one side you could see the sea almost directly below. The other looked out to a wide expanse of lawns, flowerbeds and exotic trees, with the tennis courts beyond. Within the grounds there were a few discreet shops. One of them, next to the tennis courts, was the outlet for the designs of the Caribbean's best-known tennis player, who had got to the second round at Wimbledon, and, for a Caribbean sportsman, made money.

He was the hotel's tennis coach, and during the cool times of the day could be seen moving gracefully back and forth on the courts. Altogether the place was remarkably pleasant and agreeable if you happened to be staying there. But it saddened our little party and irritated one or two. We were a small group of men who worked either in radio or on newspapers in Britain. We were all emigrants from Caribbean islands who had lived in Britain for a number of years. One or two of us had been born on this same island. All of us came from and were related to the sorts of people who cooked the food, swept the lawn, made the beds, ran the boats and walked along the sand selling small carved curios. Had we stayed in the places where we were born instead of emigrating, it is unlikely that we would ever have entered that hotel as guests. As it was we had come on a public relations trip meant for English journalists, those people from the big world who would be seeing the island and its people for the first time, as if they were tourists.

Tourists we were not. Instead, the contrast between the reality we had known as children and the world in which we now found ourselves was a painful and dislocating one.

'I wish,' said one of my friends that first night, as we stood looking out over the sea, 'that I could have brought my wife and family. She has worked so hard. She would enjoy this. She's never had a holiday like this.'

Some such thought was running through the heads of all my colleagues. From inside the hotel it was hard to believe, for a moment, that this was the same place we had lived in as children.

On the second night, we went into town to visit a couple who were said to be a focus of cultural life there. The man of the house was an Englishman and an optometrist. He explained with some care what this meant, but I can only remember a mental image of a huge pair of spectacles with nothing behind them. He had married a woman from the island in Britain and gone to live there. We were told, mysteriously, that she had been an actress, but none of us had ever seen or heard of her before. Their house also overlooked the sea. It had a beautiful view, marred only by a sign which said BEWARE DANGEROUS DOG. The front of the house was guarded by a metal grille, and when the optometrist came out to greet us he slid it aside with a grating rattle.

Shortly after we arrived, a white couple drove up in a little Volkswagen. These were natives, born on the island. Both had studied in Britain, and for the rest of the evening they told us what an unpleasant place they had found it.

Indeed, all the English we met there told us the same story. The hotel managers were an English couple who had moved to the island some twenty years before. The wife, a middle-aged blonde who dressed in a rather elaborate and stagey manner, a diamond brooch pinned to her shoulder at dinner, talked about visiting her mother in England as a sort of penance. The weather was bad, the people were rude. 'England,' she cried. 'You're welcome to it.'

None of us found this surprising. We could tell from their accents and manners that these were the sort of working-class people whose lives and work in Britain would be unlikely to be half so comfortable as appeared to be the case on the island. They were aristocracy of the town, and we couldn't help thinking that our presence must have been uncomfortable for them. Not because we were natives, but because it was reasonable to suppose that we understood very well the contrasts between their positon on the island and their place in the background they had left behind. As migrants, they were mirror images of ourselves, curiously distorted, except that, as one of the group remarked, they were doing a lot better.

On the third night, we dined together at a large table which was reserved for us every evening on the terrace. By this time we had grown accustomed to the hotel, and to some extent we were slightly bored. 'Jaundiced' is probably the word. Each day had been full of little trips, little detours to see this and that noteworthy feature of the district, endless lectures from this or that notable about the virtues of the tourist trade and the benefits of coming to the island for a holiday. I was in a mood merely to sit by myself, perhaps for the rest of the trip, gazing at the endless movement of the waves. This was Sunday night, and we would be leaving the following day.

During the weekday-nights the entertainment on the terrace consisted of a reggae band. There were about four of them, and they seemed to specialize in Bob Marley songs, full of references to injustice, particularly the injustices wreaked on black people by Babylon. Babylon, of course, was the shorthand Rastafarian term for any oppressor of black people, the rich, the whites, the owners. Authority. Babylon you soon come down, they sang. On the terrace in front of them, the guests, almost exclusively white foreigners, mainly Americans, danced with awkward delight, encouraging the band with yelps and cries and waves of their hands.

On the previous night, Saturday, this same band had played while three or four teenagers had done limbo and a fire-eating dance. Both these performances were embarrassing, because although the children were supple and athletic, their performance was really a crude and sketchy travesty of the limbo and the fire dance, neither of which was native to the island. The only boy in the group was extremely agile and handsome. He wore very tight striped trousers and had an impressive reflexive sense of rhythm, which he demonstrated by skipping pertly between two bamboo poles which the girls clashed together.

'He's only fourteen,' whispered the hotel-keeper's wife. She confided that she thought him as good as the director of the island's national dance theatre. This director, a world-famous intellectual, was also a professor at the university, and choreographed and danced with his troupe in ballets which had been presented all over the world, at such places as Sadler's Wells. The hotel-keeper's wife had seen one of their performances and conceived a high regard for the director's athleticism. So talented, she murmured. This performance, however, served merely to refresh some of our group's lurking resentments. As exiles, we had nourished a high regard for our islands' folk traditions. We were accustomed to seeing painstakingly re-created versions of such dances. The entertainment seemed a cheap, poorly conceived night-club version of folk tradition, like an ugly and slightly sadistic game, while our hostess's comparison between the agile boy and the learned professor seemed like an insult.

This Sunday was different. On the terrace were three men with guitars and drums. Their instruments were acoustic rather than electronic like the reggae groups we'd seen previously, and this wasn't the only difference in their style. The reggae band had been composed of glossy young men dressed in a fashion which would have passed without notice in Queens or Hackney or Amsterdam. Tight trousers, silk shirts, medallions, hair teased into immaculate afros or beaded, glistening dreadlocks. It would have been no surprise to see them anywhere on the sort of circuit where black bands played.

The three men on the terrace that Sunday, however, looked a bit odd, even in that setting. Seeing them made it apparent, all of a sudden, that the Jamaicans we saw in the hotel all wore uniforms of some sort. Even the clothes the reggae band had been wearing looked like a kind of uniform. This group wore the sort of clothes worn by people in the street and by men serving behind the Montego Bay bars. As if conscious of the problem, they had made one or two attempts to elevate their apparel into costume. Their leader, the singer, wore a ragged hat made of coconut fronds. Another had knotted his shirt above his midriff. They looked like scarecrows, parodies. When they appeared, we felt sympathy.

The feeling was something more than sympathy. We were stricken by a species of helplessness, a moral paralysis, very similar to what we felt when faced by the ugly stumps of a mutilated beggar in the street; and helpless, we all looked at the calypsonian among us, as if it was clear he would know what to do.

As it happened, he wasn't a calypsonian any more. He was by this time a well-known broadcaster presenting a programme which was famous among black people in Britain, and although he had left his calypsonian days far behind, he remained, as he frequently pointed out, a musician at heart. Ironically, his children had been sent to an expensive private school for young musicians where they were becoming skilled practitioners of classical music. But, as he said sometimes, he had no intention of letting his children forage as he had done. Even so, his distance from the times when he had been in the same situation as these men increased his sympathy and identity with them, and now he went over to the ragged singer and greeted him as a brother.

Later on, seated at the edge of the terrace, he told us what he had talked about with the singer. He and I were having lobster, a speciality of the hotel, and before the dish arrived he told us the musician's story, a little hurriedly as if to get the subject out of the way.

They were, of course, unemployed and the manager allowed them, on Sundays only as a concession, to play on the terrace and to keep whatever tips they received. As our food was served they began to sing, and as we had half expected they were terrible. It wasn't their voices, or the way they played their instruments. It was more their choice of songs. They began with 'Yellow Bird' and went on to 'Jamaica Farewell'. Obviously these were songs that tourists would know and regard as typical of the Caribbean, and indeed one or two of the middle-aged couples dining near us smiled and hummed with appreciation. To our ears, there was something dolorous and mournful about the sound, spiritless. In that setting there was something alien even about the lyrics – 'I left a little girl in Kingston Town.' No one ever spoke like that. Our calypsonian grimaced and smiled wryly. We prepared to ignore the music.

As we ate, the musicians circulated round the terrace, stopping to sing perfunctorily at each table and moving on when they'd been given a tip. Engaged in conversation among ourselves, we had almost forgotten about them when a voice was raised above the hubbub of dinner-table chat, cutting precisely through the air to fall on our ears as contemptuously as it must have fallen on those of the musicians.

'Go away. Don't come to this table.'

The accent was American, and it belonged to a woman sitting nearby. We had seen her, and taken notice when she arrived, partly because she was the only other black person dining on the terrace. She was with a white couple, also American by the sound of their voices, and during dinner she had appeared to be doing most of the talking. She had the serious and aggressive air typical of some black Americans, but somehow her manner made us feel a little uncomfortable. We recognized that tense, drawn face, anger barely suppressed beneath its surface, and somehow it seemed inappropriate here. It was the face with which we encountered life in Britain, giving nothing away except anger and determination. In the Caribbean we wanted our faces to be friendly, open and relaxed. This was supposed to be home. So we had looked at her and seen a foreigner, forgetting that we too were now foreigners in this place.

'Go away,' she said, speaking to the musicians as we imagined she might have addressed a beggar.

The singer stopped, his voice trailing away uncertainly, and he stood staring at her for a long moment, but the American woman had already turned away and was speaking once again to her friends. It was, we felt instinctively, that she was ashamed of what they were. Young black people of her sort in the USA had begun to support themselves by erecting a new network of self-images. In order to be worthy of respect, black men had to be strong, rebellious or at least sleek and handsome. She saw the calypsonians as humble beggars, hands outstretched for a tip from a gaggle of contemptuous whites, and it was clear that her version of self-respect demanded this cruelty.

For a moment the musicians hovered; then they began to walk away in silence. At our table there was a feeling of embarrassment and anger. It was as if we too had been humiliated and insulted there in the middle of that wide terrace. But before anyone could speak, one of our party called out to the musicians.

'Hey, come. Come and sing for us, Mr Calypsonian.'

Others at the table called out too, and after a tiny hesitation the little group turned and walked towards us, moving with a touch of sullenness. When they arrived we shook hands with them and introduced ourselves.

'I would like to try my luck in England,' the singer said.

'Sing us a real calypso,' someone asked him.

'What do you want to hear?' he asked cautiously.

'"Jean and Dinah",' I said.

It was one of the few calypsos I could remember. It was an old one, written sometime, I supposed, during the 1950s after the US naval bases sited in Trinidad had closed down and the US sailors had gone home. The calypso celebrated the fact that the local prostitutes, deprived of the Yankees' generous custom, now had to return to their Trinidadian clientele. It was a characteristic mixture of casual obscenity and defiant social comment and, as such, it remained a typical and, oddly, a more or less topical calypso.

The singer was silent for a moment, then without speaking to his fellow musicians he began to play the first bars of the song. We were prepared to sing along or encourage him in some way, to lend a little spirit to the performance, but when he started, the hangdog cadence with which he had sung previously was gone. Instead he sang with the teasing insolence and the high, full-blooded power of a true calypsonian.

Jean and Dinah, Rosita and Clementina round the corner. . . .

Opposite me our former calypsonian nodded and smirked with joy. Our tour guide, the only woman in our party, an Englishwoman who worked for the local tourist board, began to tap her spoon and sway in her seat. People turned to look.

> Bet your life is something they selling
> And if you catch them broken
> You can get it all for nothing
> Don't make no row
> Yankees gone, I take over now.

When this refrain came, the whole table howled the words with gusto. Around us the American tourists, prepared to enjoy everything although they could not have understood the words, were looking at us with broad smiles. The black American woman, however, was still talking, resolutely ignoring us, and as I looked, she and her companions got up to leave.

The song came to an end, and when someone at the table called out 'Benwood Dick', the singer, warm now, launched into the refrain without stopping.

> Hey lil boy let me tell you this
> Don't be afraid I am not the police. . . .

By this time we were all in the grip of a joy approaching hysteria. The little band had been transformed. The singer stood, legs apart, chest thrown out; his friends the drummer and marimba player seemed to have caught his mood and the rhythm of their playing had become so fierce and precise that we couldn't help banging the table, tapping our glasses and dancing in our seats. Around the edges of the terrace the waiters paused, grinning, and the receptionists crowded in to look.

> . . . tell your sister to come down
> Quick I have something here for she
> Tell she is Mr Benwood Dick the man from Sande Grande.

Under cover of the noise, our calypsonian explained the words to our guide, who blushed and grinned, then waved her fist at him when he winked at us. Everyone laughed. It was the first time we had felt so friendly towards her.

The music came to an end. 'I got to move around now,' the singer said.

We each handed in the money for his tip, and our calypsonian gave it to him. He couldn't have seen such good pickings for some time, I thought uncharitably. He shook hands before moving away.

'I really appreciated the way you listened to my music,' he said awkwardly.

'We appreciated it too,' I said.

He walked away, only going as far as two tables distant. Soon he started to sing, the same song with which he had begun the evening, and in the same subdued tone: 'Yellow bird, high up in banana tree.'

In front of him the Americans swayed and nodded, even though the little band sounded as listless as it had done previously.

'Bloody hell,' muttered the man seated next to me. He had been born in a village nearby, but had gone to live in North London at the age of ten. This was his first trip back. 'Bloody hell,' he said. 'This is a good place for a visit, but I wouldn't like to live here.'

Cuba: Que Linda (1978)

Moise was my personal interpreter. But that wasn't an official post. By no means. We already had two interpreters, teenage girls who studied languages at the university and who frequently reduced Jimmy, the *Mirror* man, to a state of incoherent rage. Whenever something went wrong, as it did every morning, Jimmy would shoot impatient questions at them, getting redder and angrier by the second. They were terrified of him anyway, and when this happened their English would almost entirely desert them. At these times, the younger of the pair, Maria, would fall back on the only English phrase she could remember, and in answer to every question or enquiry, would reply in a small voice, 'More or less.'

Jimmy maintained that we shouldn't stand for it. He felt that the fact we'd been given these two 'incompetents', as he often called them, meant that our status with the Cubans was extremely low. Privately we all agreed, but few of us cared, and we certainly didn't want to encourage him in any gung-ho crap like writing a letter of protest to the authorities, an action at which he hinted a couple of times. In any case this was a soft trip. The man from the *Guardian* had brought his wife, and most of us were in a holiday mood. People from the dailies felt pressed to file a few lines every couple of days, but even that was to slacken off as the week wore on, and attendance at the daily press conferences grew sporadic.

Even so, as Jimmy pointed out from time to time, it was clear that our colleagues from the socialist countries had first pick of all the stories. They even got to see Fidel in the first days. But, as Peter, the man from *The Times* pointed out, none of this mattered very much, because most of our papers only expected the odd filler from this lot, and most of us had wangled the trip because we were interested in the event and fancied going to Cuba. Indeed, if the Festival of Youth and Students hadn't been taking place in Havana, few of us, except for the man from the *Morning Star*, would have been allowed to go. But then, in the late 1970s, revolutionary Cuba was still *terra incognita* for Western reporters, and any excuse, even a Commie front, as Jimmy called it, was worth taking up, just to get into the country.

So we found ourselves trailing a group of 'young people' and looking for a story. Only about half of them were students; the other half came from community organizations and projects – feminist groups, law centres, advice centres, left-wing parties – Commie sympathizers, Jimmy called them.

These made up the British delegation to which we were attached. Most had come to worship at the revolutionary shrine, and they made it plain they regarded the press and press people as objects of deep suspicion, hyenas. We, the hacks, reciprocated with amusement, and in any case, we hardly noticed their hostility because we were staying, as the authorities directed, in a hotel reserved for the press in the centre of Havana, while the delegation was billeted in a college situated miles away from the town. Besides, we had problems of our own. It was second nature for most of the hacks immediately to set about matters of accreditation, opening lines of communication with the paper, and collecting as much information as possible about press conferences, special events and so on. Not to do so would have been a transgression, sinful. Everyone had the superstitious feeling that if you neglected these matters, something astonishingly newsworthy would happen while you lazed around in total ignorance, or with no access to any of the facilities you needed.

None of this was easy. The procedures turned out to be almost incredibly bureaucratic, and the bureaucracy turned out to be numbingly cumbersome. This wasn't ill-will on the part of the organizers. They did, after all, provide access and transport to all the major events and press conferences. There were trips to factories and revolutionary monuments, films, plays, sporting events. On the other hand, the British hacks assumed that whatever we were allowed to see would be something the authorities wanted us to see. No one wanted to spend their time writing down the platitudes of a succession of Communist worthies, and most of the events to which we had access were useful only for colour and background pieces. We were looking for facilities which would allow us to find out things for ourselves. This made matters difficult. For instance, in the case of transport Jimmy wanted a minibus, like the Russians, so that we could go wherever we wished. He made his demand on the second day, talking his way into the office of the press director and confronting him with a list of shortcomings in the facilities. He emerged triumphant. The director had listened to him and promised he would try to do something the following day.

'The sucker's dreaming,' I muttered to *The Times* man.

This was a Caribbean country. I had realized that from the moment we'd landed and seen the customs men jigging and swaying to the music coming over the public address system. I could imagine what the organizers would do when faced with a sweating, red-faced white man, threatening, irate and making impossible demands. Mañana. They'd promise him what he wanted – tomorrow. I understood this, because underneath the trappings of the revolution there was something achingly familiar about almost everything in the country. The people looked just like people in Trinidad or Jamaica – more or less half of them seemed to be black, and a good many of the other half were a characteristic mixture of races. When I walked down the street alone, people often spoke to me in Spanish, and I soon realized that there was little or nothing to distinguish me from the average Cuban. Partly, perhaps, for this reason, I began to feel a kind of defensiveness about my colleagues' irritability. In the beginning, for instance, they grumbled continually about the fact that everywhere they went they encountered officials, guards, committee chairmen, custodians of this and that and the other. In front of the lift on each floor of our hotel was a desk where someone sat, presumably checking people with no legitimate business in the building.

'They're watching us,' someone said. 'Everybody's watching someone else in these countries.'

'They're no different to the porters or receptionists who hang around the front desk of the paper,' I argued, but they wouldn't be convinced.

As it happened, the girl at the desk on our floor had spoken to me the day before. When I said hello to her, she'd asked me whether I came from Jamaica. Her grandfather, she told me, came from that country, and he had taught them to speak English. She was just about to enter university, and one day she wanted to go to Jamaica. She might well have been one of my sisters, I thought, and it was odd and unpleasant to hear her being talked about as if she were some sort of hard-faced commissar.

By this time we'd established a routine. We'd start the day by going to a press conference or an interview. It was important to do this as early as possible because later on it would simply be too hot. We seemed to have struck the hottest part of the year, and moving around during the day was difficult. Even well before noon, I'd be dripping with sweat when I returned to the hotel.

We were staying at the Havana Libre, which was once the Hilton and was still furnished appropriately. It was easy to imagine it before the revolution. During the hottest hours of the day we sat in the poolside bar, behind which a smiling barman dispensed a seemingly endless variety of rum cocktails.

Nothing, however, could dispel the feeling of incongruity about being in that hotel. I had, of course, been to desperately poor countries before and found myself staying in the lap of luxury. That wasn't new. I had also been in places which felt like enclaves for tourists or for the press, and there was nothing strange about that either. What was unusual was the sense that the building was a sort of archaic museum, carefully preserved for the use of foreigners, and functioning just as it had done in the days of the old regime. The dining-room, for instance, was a huge, echoing place at the top of the building, where I went with Peter, *The Times* man. Usually we were the only people there, apart from a small party of silent Russians, who sat in front of the piano. This was a gleaming grand piano which looked as if it belonged on the concert stage, and was manned by a middle-aged Cuban in shirt-sleeves who sang old American ballads in a lugubrious voice. It was like being in a 1950s movie – the crooning tones of the singer, the Russians grunting softly with approval, the rows and rows of empty tables around us. Peter said it was like being in an English seaside hotel. But it was hard to believe that anything else could have the same archaic, intensely preserved air.

Later on, when I asked Moise about this, he looked puzzled. 'The foreigners like it,' he said. He shrugged. I didn't pursue the question, because he had a way of losing interest in some issues that you could see in the change of his expression, as if a light had gone out behind his eyes. Of course, I hadn't spotted this side of him at first. On the contrary, it was his easy style which caught my attention. I was walking along the street one evening in the first week when I literally bumped into Moise. 'Sorry,' I said automatically, to which he replied, 'OK. No problem.' He sounded vaguely American, and I assumed that he was from the English-speaking Caribbean. Bermuda perhaps. I had spent the previous evening with a student from Guyana and some of his friends, and they all, I thought, had a sort of carefree air which marked them out from the Cubans whom I met. After all, they were far away from home, with no family obligations, and no pressures except the need to finish their courses. Some saw it as a long-extended holiday.

In contrast, Cuban students had to account to neighbourhood committees, revolutionary councils and government watchdogs of various kinds. Visitors from other parts of the Caribbean felt irresponsible in comparison, and admired their seriousness without wanting to emulate it. In any case the students I met from countries like Guyana, Jamaica or Grenada carried themselves in a way that was markedly different from their Cuban colleagues.

When I turned round and saw Moise that evening I assumed he was a foreign student. Perhaps it was the easy way he brushed aside my apologies, or perhaps it was the fluency of his English. Without thinking about it, I asked him which island he came from. He laughed. 'I'm Cuban,' he said. 'Cuban through and through.'

I asked him where he had learned his English and he told me he was a student at the university. He had tried to get a summer job he said, as an interpreter, but he hadn't been successful. This seemed odd when I compared his English to that of our two translators, but I thought it might embarrass him if I mentioned it. Instead I asked him to come into the hotel for a drink. He accepted immediately. Like any Caribbean twenty-year-old it seemed he was simply hanging out, and was ready to go anywhere that caught his interest.

That evening by coincidence there was a cabaret at the hotel.

Since seeing the lunchtime entertainment, both Peter and I had been fascinated by the prospect, and we weren't disappointed. The Russians arrived early, a little more noisy than usual and plainly in a mood to be entertained. Jimmy, looking for good quotes, was ensconced in a corner with a few of them, buying bottles of vodka. Peter and I sat with Moise, who told us that it would be the sort of show foreigners used to enjoy in Havana before the revolution.

In the event it seemed to be precisely that. As the band wound up into a samba it was easy to imagine the corrupt Yankees and Mafia godfathers rolling up in the shark-finned American cars, which, covered in transfers and peeling neon paint, served as taxis throughout the city. The band itself was dressed in the ruffled shirts and sashes which signalled Latin America in the old movies, and as they played, the dancers who moved onto the huge stage all looked like versions of Carmen Miranda, with tall head-dresses made of feathers and fruit, carried around on long, long legs. They sang and danced exactly like a Hollywood musical, one of those where Bing Crosby and Bob Hope are flying down to Rio, and the band bristled with maracas and cha-cha-cha.

But the oddest feature was that almost all the chorus-girls were middle-aged. There was something bizarre about watching them prancing and skipping, wide grins of effort on their sweating faces.

'Why are they so old?' I asked Moise.

He shrugged. These were artists of the former times, he said. Nowadays the girls who wanted to be dancers went in for ballet or folkloric training. These were the last of the showgirls.

Later on I went for a walk with Moise. It was Saturday night and the entire town seemed to be in a holiday mood. Carnival was coming soon, and every street corner seemed to shriek with the music of trumpets and vibrated with drums. Somehow the atmosphere reminded me again of New York. Spanish Harlem was exactly like this – the massive queues waiting for the buses, the patient women and children, the rows of youths squatting on the pavements, like birds on a telegraph line. Out of the darkness a hissing staccato – mira, mira.

Ahead of us, two Russians stepped off the pavement and hailed their minibus which was cruising slowly up the road as if looking for them. We could tell they were Russians because they were white and had that sort of blocky look they all seemed to have. When the minibus stopped, they got in and drove away without looking back. From the pavement the people watched them in the way I'd seen other Caribbeans watch European tourists in other places, with a peculiar mixture of envy and contempt.

In New York, and maybe Jamaica or Barbados, they'd have been mugged, I told Moise. He looked amazed.

'That's what would happen,' I said, 'to any foreigner who looked rich or had things we didn't.'

'No,' Moise said, 'that wouldn't happen here. They are our only friends in the world outside. They come here to help us.'

'It doesn't matter,' I said. I began telling him about mugging, but he'd already been told such things. It was inevitable in such decadent societies, he said, that people should vent their frustration on foreign exploiters and the callous rich. I told him about a recent mugging in Barbados, in which an elderly Canadian, out for a walk, had been stopped by a gang of youths. They'd searched him and found no money, until one of them had the bright idea of looking in his shoes. After they'd taken the money they found in there, the gang cut both of his feet across the middle of the soles. 'Next time,' they said, 'don't try and fool us.'

Moise's expression was horrified. Like the rest of his contemporaries he was a part-time soldier. He could operate a variety of weapons and devices which would kill and maim, and if the Yankees invaded, he said, he expected to be in the forefront of the fighting. But the violence I had described shocked him. For a little while he was silent, and to change the subject I asked him about the local posadas. The students I met had told me about them at some length. It was the same back home, they said, and all over most of Latin America. Housing was scarce, and almost all young people who were unmarried lived at home with their parents; even married people who lived with their parents, sisters and brothers sometimes needed privacy for their intimate moments. This was what the Guyanese students called fuckhouses. When I told Jimmy, he almost crowed with delight. Over the past few years he had made a special study of Eastern brothels, and wanted to expand his efforts into the West. He told us about brothels in Bangkok where a paper he worked for had an account, and where visiting executives were taken immediately they arrived. In this place girls sat behind a one-way mirror and the customers summoned them by number.

'It's nothing of that kind,' I said. 'It's just a convenience.'

'It would be useful though,' he said thoughtfully, 'to get a shot of them queuing up outside one.'

To amuse Moise I told him what Jimmy had said, and he laughed heartily as we walked along. From time to time he'd see a friend, and they would hold up their hands in greeting like a black power salute, with the palms open instead of a closed fist. The clubbiness of the greeting and the number of young people whom Moise greeted like this gave me a strange feeling. Until the age of puberty I had grown up with boys and girls I'd known from birth. We'd shared the same experiences, the same memories, for all that time. Then I had left to live in Britain, and the people I knew became boys towards whom I felt distant or hostile. Even the people I knew and liked best were, at a certain level, strangers. Moise must have had no idea of what it was like to live in such an alien landscape, and for a moment I envied him intensely.

The next evening we went to a concert being staged near the old cathedral. Moise met me at the hotel and we walked there. We were early because we would have had to walk there anyway, and he wanted to show me various parts of the town. As we moved away from the seafront and down towards the older part of Havana, the character of the buildings began to change. Instead of the tall oblongs of concrete and glass, we began to go past elegant Hispanic shapes – rose-coloured plaster, peeling stucco and slender, fluted columns. The street became narrower, and we kept on having to squeeze past families standing or sitting on the pavement in front of their houses, or leaning out of the flat-fronted jalousie windows. As we walked down one street a middle-aged man at the centre of one of these family groups waved and called out to Moise. 'My cousin,' he said, and we stopped to talk. The man, dressed in a singlet, trousers and sneakers, spoke rapidly to Moise and then said something to me. My Spanish still wasn't good enough to understand, and I looked at Moise for translation. He smiled and said something in reply. I caught the word 'delegado'. The man threw open the door of his house with a flourish of his wrist: 'Bienvenido.' We entered, followed by four small children. The house was really a tiny flat, full of the jumble of accumulated living – beds, a table, a TV set in one corner, and in the other corner a cotton-haired old lady in a dilapidated armchair. Roberto, Moise's cousin, produced two straight-backed chairs with the same hospitable flourish and we sat down. He offered me a cigar and we talked, with Moise translating most of the time. Roberto had something to do with making cigars, a good job, and he wanted to know if I was enjoying my visit. It was nice to see the foreigners, he said, who came to support them in their struggles against poverty and the Yankees. I nodded and smiled, turned down a meal and accepted a glass of rum. He reminded me of my uncle Aubrey, and this house with its overcrowded, dingy air and its homely smells reminded me of a house in the street where I was born. So I asked him what were the difficulties of being black in this country. I put the question to Moise because my Spanish wasn't equal to the task, and he gave me a surprised look. I could understand his surprise, partly because I hadn't raised the question with him, which was a little odd considering that we were two young black men meeting for the first time in a place that was strange to one of us. Anywhere else it would have been an obvious enquiry, like English people talking about the weather, and perhaps I hadn't made it before because the country didn't feel like a white man's country in the way that England or Canada or the USA does. But talking to Roberto made me remember something that an old black sailor had told me in New York about sailing to Cuba in the 1930s and 1940s in the high days of the Yankees and their dictators. It was like a concentration camp for black people, he'd said. 'They lived behind barbed wire. Yes, I saw it. In Havana I never liked going ashore.' This was a tough old man who smuggled packages ('they never told me what it was') for the mobsters all through the war. Something of the seamed lines of Roberto's face had triggered off that memory and prompted my question.

Moise paused as if he had to work out how to put it, and when Roberto heard the question, he too hesitated for a moment, and when he spoke he looked directly at me.

'The past,' Moise translated, 'is difficult to describe and painful to remember. Before the revolution you could be one of three things, a boxer, a bongo player or a labourer. Now I know of blacks who are such things as doctors or economists.' He paused, then said something else, and Moise, instead of translating, replied in Spanish. Roberto repeated the phrase with an impatient gesture of his fingers, and this time I got it before Moise put it into English – 'nothing is perfect.'

By the time we entered the square where the concert was to be held, we were feeling cheerful, if not entirely sober, and I was in the mood to be impressed, but I wasn't prepared for the sheer charm of the setting. I'd seen squares like this before in the Hispanic parts of the Caribbean, a characteristic mixture of grandeur and shabbiness. The cathedral closed off one end of the square, and the old stone steps made up a huge stage, overlooked by the upper storeys of the houses around the other three sides.

We arrived late, and on the cathedral steps the dancers were winding slow, intricate figures. It was, Moise explained, part of a ballet which celebrated the island's African heritage. We'd already missed most of it, and we missed the rest looking for a place from which we could see properly over the heads of the people massed in the centre of the square. Eventually Moise turned and led the way through the columns at the side of the square and down a narrow alley. The sound of the drums faded and grew muffled as we went, but Moise pressed on confidently into the dark. Soon we were climbing up a winding iron staircase like a fire-escape, and then Moise opened a door which led into a flat where two women, a man and several small children were looking out of the windows. Moise talked fast, with a lot of smiles and gestures. I heard the word 'delegado' and in a moment we emerged onto a balcony almost immediately overlooking the cathedral steps, from which we watched the rest of the performance.

The next act was just coming on, a Cuban band which sounded

like salsa, the sort of music you could hear belting out of attics and cellars in Manhattan, Saturday night PR music. It was greeted with enthusiasm and delight by the crowd, singing along with the lyrics, and oohing and aahing at the screaming pyrotechnics of the trumpet player. After it was over the applause was loud and prolonged.

On the balcony we made conversation. The occupants of the flat asked me whether I was enjoying my visit. The man told me that the next band came from my country, Jamaica. I didn't bother correcting him, and he pointed out some Jamaicans in the crowd. They had been the ones jigging about and cheering the music louder than anyone else. In their bushy Afros, gold chains, rings and wrist-watches they looked sleek and prosperous compared with the Cubans around them.

Similarly the glossiness of the Jamaican band looked bizarre. They sang a number of songs associated with Bob Marley, full of references to Rastafari, Babylon and rebellion. The audience's response seemed merely polite, and they looked most enthusiastic when a song came up that sounded vaguely like American soul music. I had the sense that they were puzzled by more than the unfamiliar reggae rhythms. The musicians wiggled around and made obscene gestures from time to time with their hips and guitars, but their studied rebelliousness and iconoclasm left the crowd cold. I wondered why it hadn't occurred to the band that the adolescent postures of teenage rebels might bore an audience which was living its own revolution. The audience began to chatter, and people drifted away along the edges of the square. As if in answer, the band launched into its final number, which ended in a sort of rehearsed hysteria, with smoke bombs and thunder flashes going off, the guitar player systematically bashing his instrument against the speakers, gradually smashing it to pieces. Around me the faces grew horrified. 'Why is he doing that?' Moise asked me. I tried to explain, but as I talked he looked sterner and more disapproving. Down below, the crowd muttered unhappily. I suspected that for a people who went through a lifetime of making do, recycling and lovingly preserving functional artefacts, the sight of a man smashing a valuable musical instrument must have been almost traumatic. Leaving the square I felt slightly embarrassed – exposed.

Moise himself didn't comment, although during the following week I had plenty of opportunity to observe the same reaction at work over some of our foreigners' antics. For instance, on the evening I took Moise along to a party for delegados, several people stripped off and ran into the sea. To Moise such a display was blatant, and also puzzling, since the frolicsome nudists did nothing except to put their clothes back on and go home. He had disappeared for an hour or so into the bushes with a Dutch girl, and he found it odd that the naked couples hadn't done something similar. 'I like foreigners,' he said, 'but they're crazy.'

By this time I saw very little of our interpreters. I was still puzzled by the fact that Moise, whose English was so good, had been unable to get a job as a translator while our official interpreters spoke such poor English. So I was pleased when, out walking one day with Moise, we met Maria, the younger and prettier of the two girls. I called out to her, and she came up, smiling with pleasure. I introduced her to Moise, and she said that they had seen each other at the university, but she was a year behind him. It was the first time they had talked. Moise seemed a little reserved at first, but they were soon chatting happily. It was obvious that they liked each other, and they made a good-looking couple: Maria with her fair curly hair and lithe, slender build, Moise a slim, athletic youth with strong, graceful movements. Before we parted she gave Moise her telephone number and address, and as we moved away she bestowed on him a lingering smile, eyelashes down, the look that Hispanic Caribbean women could use with devastating effect.

'Will you see her?' I asked Moise.

He shrugged.

'Perhaps I'll visit her.' He paused, his face serious. 'But just as a friend.'

'Come on, Moise,' I said. 'The girl likes you.'

He shrugged again and hesitated. 'She's white,' he said eventually. 'Maybe her parents won't like it.'

'I thought,' I told him with a little touch of sarcasm, 'that the revolution had done away with all of that.'

'In a way,' he replied seriously. 'But there are many of the old elements still here in our society. Fidel has mentioned it many times in his speeches, but it's not easy to change people so quickly.'

He didn't mention the subject again, although we talked many times afterwards about being black in the USA and Britain, and about the history of the African people and culture in Cuba.

When our trip came to an end and we were due to leave, Lucia and Maria, our interpreters, came with us in our official minibus to the airport. Somehow Moise had made his own way there, and as we disembarked to go through customs I saw him coming towards me, jaunty as ever, holding out his present, some cigars carefully wrapped in paper. Lucia and Maria had already given us presents on the bus, and they had sobbed and looked downcast all the way, creating an almost tangible atmosphere of guilt among the press party about our bad temper during the previous fortnight. Looking back from the plane I can still remember Moise with one arm around each of the weeping girls, all three of them waving from time to time.

Months later in London I got a postcard from him, but there was no address so I couldn't write back, and years after that I was invited to a reception for a new Cuban ambassador, who turned out to be a black man. After several rums it was my turn to shake the ambassador's hand and converse. I asked him whether he knew my friend Moise, but he was from a different part of the country and had never heard of him.

— 9 —

Such a Nice Kid

A Story of Academic Life
in the USA (1982)

A little while after we took off, I ordered bourbon. I had begun drinking bourbon during my first journeys to the USA and now I always drank it on planes. It made me feel light and relaxed – in a holiday mood. This time I felt even more cheerful than usual, because this was a working trip. My fare would be paid, and I'd be returning with money in my pocket. 'Nice one,' I muttered to myself, thinking about it. To cap it all I'd be in Boston, with Kate. Perfect.

I was feeling so good that when the plane came in over Logan I looked out calmly and without dread at the wreckage of the plane which had crashed there only a few months before. That had been during the winter, and I'd flown in two days after it had happened, trying, during the plane's descent, to persuade myself that I wasn't apprehensive. Now, in the summer sunshine, the fears of that gloomy day seemed laughable.

In this mood I strolled through the ritual of passports and customs. In comparison with JFK, getting through Logan Airport was quick and easy. In a flash, it seemed, I was out of the airport and standing on the subway platform. It was a good feeling, because everything was so reassuringly familiar. It was odd, I thought, that coming here felt like coming home. By contrast, although I'd lived in England for thirty years, child and man, I always felt tense and worried going back there.

I emerged in Harvard Square, which was, as is usual in the spring and summer, littered with students. They always looked the same. Regardless of changes in style and fashion these students seemed indistinguishable from the ones I'd seen in previous years. In one corner of the square two boys were playing the guitar and singing. I walked past them through the university yard. More students, snatches of soul music from the open windows. I slowed down, lingering over the sense that I was in a place I loved, the trees, the softening sunlight, the warm gleam of the stone buildings.

Kate's flat was the lower half of a house on the other side of the campus. The street was lined with these houses, mostly made of wood, lined with shingles and balconies. In the village where I grew up these were the sorts of houses found in more prosperous areas, with a paling fence and a backyard, an alley-way running through to the garage at the back.

The key was, as usual, under a log at the bottom of the stairs. I opened the door and went in, through the book-lined living room, into the kitchen, where I got out the coffee and started brewing it. The next step was to turn on the radio, tuned to the student station, which played reggae and soul all day. All that done, I fell onto the sofa and rang Kate. I got her secretary, who told me that she was giving a lecture. I told her that I was at the flat. She told me to have a nice day.

I was sleeping when Kate came in. I had met her at a conference a couple of years previously, and we'd been close ever since, with one of us travelling to England or the USA at least twice a year. This time she'd managed to arrange a couple of lectures for me, and we both hoped that I could earn enough money to make the frequent journeys less painful.

She'd begun talking from the moment she came through the door. She had been teaching at the university for about two years, and they would soon be deciding whether or not she got tenure. The process was long and complex, and involved being assessed by students, colleagues and the university authorities. Kate, as she usually did, described the detail of the political alliances and arguments, which had been taking place over the previous months. The support of her department was now firm and she had begun to direct her efforts towards the position of department head. She mentioned a historian, whose support she was anxious to gain.

'He's coming to your lecture,' she said casually.

'Oh, God,' I groaned. 'Can't you put him off?'

'Rubbish,' she said. 'You're going to be very good. Do me a lot of credit.'

I wasn't sure about this but there was little to be done now. I was going to talk about the politics of the British Left, and up to that point I hadn't taken the whole business very seriously. A couple of my lectures would be to undergraduate classes, and that wouldn't take any preparation, because as the conventional wisdom went, undergraduates generally knew so little that my remarks wouldn't have to be very erudite. The lecture at which the historian would be present, however, was something altogether different. I'd be addressing a research group which specialized in Left politics, most of them Kate's colleagues. If I made a mess of it, Kate's stock would inevitably go down. I was about to ask her who else would be present at the lecture but she firmly changed the subject.

'Alvarez and Maria are coming tonight,' she said. 'They're finishing their book. He lost his post at the university, and they're trying to get a job in California, so he's writing like a maniac and she's hitting up everyone who can do something for them. It's touch and go, though, because the right wing is really mobilizing to block people on the Left being recruited.'

Kate had mentioned Alvarez and Maria before, although I'd never met them. But the profile was familiar. They had written a number of commentaries on the work of French and Italian Marxists, and had in recent years been engaged in a number of ideological disputes with the Communist Party, the Spanish government and various academics around the world. Many of Kate's friends had similar biographies and similar problems. Sometimes, looking at her, I found it difficult to believe she was involved with such people. It wasn't that I was in any doubt about her intellectual ability or her interest in politics. It was just at these times, when she tossed her black curls and grinned across half her face, she looked so unreasonably youthful for a woman in her late thirties, her expression carefree and untroubled by thought or anger. I supposed that this was something to do with being American. She ski'd in winter and in the summer she went to the Caribbean or California. During the weekends, she and her friends sometimes went hiking, full of vigour and excitement. In between these times, she worked on her third book, sat on various committees, attended dance classes, wrote for a number of journals and lived a social life full of cooking, dinner parties and argument. In comparison, I felt tired and listless. Perhaps, I had often thought, that was something to do with living in England.

Alvarez was a tall, stocky man with a greying beard. Maria was small and perky. After dinner they talked about their book, and about the chances of getting work. I found my attention drifting continually, but I woke up a little when I realized they were talking about England. Alvarez had spent a couple of months there 'studying the situation'. But he had no hope for the place.

'There is no real progress in England,' he said. 'The domination of the Right is complete, and they have now captured the whole apparatus of state power.'

Kate eyed me with something challenging in her expression, but I decided not to take the bait. Alvarez, I guessed, was talking about the prospects for revolutionary change. At the same time, there was something a little irritating about his dismissive tone.

'I agree with you,' Kate told me later on after her friends had left. 'He doesn't understand the nature of change in Britain. You should have said so.'

I shrugged. The argument hadn't been worth the energy, I thought. But that wasn't a sentiment Kate would find sympathetic. So I changed the subject by asking her what the general feeling was in the research group about recent developments in England. She looked at me apologetically.

'No feeling at all. Well, Baker's interested, but he's an Anglophile. Most people here are into Spain or Italy or one of the Latin American countries. The trouble with England is that the structures aren't accessible. You have to think English to be in sympathy with them. I don't know what it is. The class system or something makes the English more involved with each other than they are with ideas or ideology or anything you can understand or be engaged with from the outside. A socialist municipality in Italy where you can meet people who understand politics and live the process is a lot more fun.'

'Hah,' I grunted. 'How the hell am I going to rival these guys from the Continent?'

'They don't have a tad of your charm,' she said.

Later on we watched *Casablanca* on TV. This was one of the things I loved about being in the USA – watching classic movies in the early morning. Kate too loved 1940s movies and movie style. Somewhere she'd got hold of a selection of cards featuring actors like Bogart, George Raft and Lauren Bacall, and she'd send them to me one by one. Sometimes she'd post two in one day, with cryptic messages like 'arrest the usual suspects' or 'you do know how to whistle?' All these meant she wanted me to ring her.

Half-way through the movie, after Claude Rains had gone through one of his exchanges with Bogart, I told her about one of the thoughts that had slipped in and out of my consciousness earlier on.

'You know, academics in England wouldn't be in the least bit interested in what I thought or had to say about English politics. They might if I was talking about being black, but not about anything else.'

'Not unless you were Stuart Hall,' she said. She turned and looked at me smiling. She understood what I meant, but she couldn't resist challenging an inaccuracy.

'Okay,' I said, 'but they only allow one Stuart at a time.'

Next day we drove to New York. I was due to meet Hugh, who was an assistant professor at a college in Brooklyn where I would be addressing a class. We started late, because Kate's car had been towed away in the morning. The parking system was complex, one side of the road on alternate days, the other side during the rest of the week. When she forgot, they'd tow the car away, and this time it was early afternoon before she got the car back and we could set off.

Kate's car was an old Chevy. Some time previously I'd known a black car hop in New York who had a Chevy of approximately the same make and age, but while he had meant to get rid of the old heap as soon as possible and buy a shiny new Mustang, Kate was inordinately fond of her car. I think she saw it as a piece of Americana, an antique, like a nineteenth-century quilt.

We didn't get into the city until the evening and we went straight to the restaurant where we were to meet Hugh and his wife. I had first run into Hugh in London. He had written a book about the riots in Britain in 1981. He looked like an overgrown college boy, and I had liked his straightforward, friendly manner. Now, walking into the restaurant, I was pleased to see him. I had read his article, which was direct and explanatory, the work of a journalist rather than a sociologist, and I complimented him on it. His wife, Jane, listened silently. She was pretty, with long, brown hair and a well-built body just softening into middle age. Her slow, maternal smile came and went while Hugh described how his colleagues and friends had responded to the article. Afterwards she asked Kate about herself.

As it turned out, Hugh's brother also taught at a college in Boston. Hugh had been born there, and the whole family often visited Connecticut together. The evening stretched out over the small talk. Hugh began telling me about a project in the South Bronx.

'Every major politician has been there, and all of them were shocked and all of them promised the cameras to regenerate the area.'

Jane laughed. 'Reagan went there,' she said.

'The only work anyone's done,' Hugh said, 'is these little projects. I know it's a drop in the ocean. There's a lot of criticisms to be made, but at least it's action.'

Kate asked him about the man who ran the project. He was an ex-con, Hugh said, who had been born in the South Bronx, and after his release had returned, commandeered some buildings, and then, with the aid of a grant from the city, had moved in families, repaired the dwellings, and now provided a sort of sheltered environment in the middle of the devastated and abandoned area.

'He knew how to kick ass,' Hugh said. 'I only got involved because I think these people are probably the only hope for the city.'

He had taken off his glasses, and his eyes shone with enthusiasm. Jane watched him with a hint of an indulgent smile. 'The guy's really impressive,' she said.

Before we left we arranged to visit the South Bronx next day with Hugh. As we drove towards the Village, I asked Kate what she'd thought of the couple.

'I liked them,' she said. She paused for a moment, thinking. 'Hugh's kind of a type. The bumbling manner, his enthusiasm, his white shoes. He probably went to one of the big private schools, then Harvard. A well-off guy from a well-off family.' She paused again. 'She's not so classy.'

I looked at Kate. She was smiling reflectively. It was on the tip of my tongue to say that she had gone the same route as Hugh, and he treated her, I thought, with a familiarity, mingled with social defer-ence, that indicated his recognition of her as a fellow WASP yuppie. I didn't say it, because I knew that would irritate her whether or not it was true. We had an agreement. My visits were so short and so expensive that it was best to avoid points of conflict, irritability, the sort of wrangling that usually went on between couples. Instead, we agreed we should be nice to each other. Sometimes it was a strain, but usually it worked.

The apartment in which we were to stay belonged to yet another friend of Kate's who taught at the university and was away for the weekend. It was at the top of a block which towered above the square and was approached through an ornamental plaza. At the entrance to the courtyard, two uniformed men checked the credentials of visitors and residents, and one of them handed Kate a key after she'd identified herself.

Inside, the apartment was huge, a thickly carpeted expanse, big enough for a family, although there was only one bedroom, which was about the size of my flat in London. One entire wall was glass through which we could see the city laid out, a map of lights. At first the open feel of the place gave me an insecure sensation like being perched half-way up a cliff, but as I got used to it the view seemed exciting, marvellous.

Kate was in the middle of writing a lecture and she spread herself out at a table while I watched TV. Sitting in a pool of light, frowning intently and making notes from the books in front of her, she looked angular and serious, every inch the professor. Suddenly she looked up, and, seeing me looking at her from across the room, grinned widely and slammed down her pen.

'Bedtime,' she said. 'Let's go fool around.'

Next morning I woke up to the sound of Kate cursing in the kitchen. 'Assholes,' she shouted. 'Dirty mothers,' she yelled. In the kitchen she was toasting bagels and grilling bacon. She had gone out to buy breakfast. She usually started the morning by drinking a concoction of which the main ingredients were orange juice, raw eggs and a special mixture of cereals. She'd gone out to get these when she discovered that the car had been broken into during the night. Her stereo and some tapes of rare jazz performances had been taken.

'The stereo I don't mind,' she said angrily. 'But I can't replace those tapes. No way . . . Those guys were real assholes to take the tapes.'

About mid-afternoon we met Hugh on the East Side. In the car Kate told him about the stereo. It was probably, he said cheerfully, a bunch of kids who specialized in stereos.

After a while we began going past abandoned and burned-out houses. At first there would just be one or two, then as we went on, every house in every block was empty and black with the scorched remains of fire. It was a picture of complete devastation, a ruined city, flattened and reduced to rubble.

'Twenty years ago,' said Hugh, 'this was a thriving district, factories, everything. It's almost too neat an illustration of urban decline. First the industry goes and the area becomes poorer. Poorer people move in and the better-off move out. The area becomes even poorer. Housing decays. Poorer people move in. The better landlords move out. Housing decays even more. The landlords give up on repairs and improvements. The tenants give up on rent. Then a bunch of weasels start burning the houses for the insurance and it becomes a fashion, and before you know it you've got the South Bronx. Same thing's happening in New Jersey.'

The project, when we arrived there, was like an oasis, a raft in a sea of crumbling brick and twisted metal. In any other part of the city the blocks of apartments, with their fire-escapes and dustbins out front, would have seemed unremarkable.

The organizer of the project, Steve, was a large black man with a clean-shaven head and a laconic, amused manner. 'Hey, my man,' he greeted Hugh.

His coolness and size made Hugh look jerky and uncoordinated, a puppy in white shoes. They shook hands and grinned at each other with genuine warmth. Steve looked interested when Hugh introduced me.

'All the way from England huh? Nothing like this in England.' He indicated the area with a sweep of his hand, like a ruler outlining his domain. He turned to his assistant, a plump black woman who stood a little way behind him clutching a sheaf of papers. 'This guy from England.'

'No shit,' she said. 'Hi.'

'You from England too?' he asked Kate.

She shook her head. 'No, Boston.'

'Boston, huh?' His manner became a little more reserved, and he turned and led us into one of the apartment blocks, already talking about vandalism, block democracy, the problems of cooperative shopping and protecting the apartments from squatters and bandits. It seemed that his day consisted of one long round of armed caretaking duties.

Back in his office he showed us a map of the area, with the project marked by a small red dot. Soon they would be taking over another block. A drop in the ocean, I thought. I had also been impressed by Steve's energy and optimism, so I could understand Hugh's enthusiasm about him, but the notion of regenerating the district from this tiny base seemed ludicrously unrealistic.

Steve must have seen something in my face because he nodded at me wryly. 'Only another few hundred acres to go, huh? I know it looks kind of impossible, but everyone else has quit, except the priest down the road, and he's going to quit before I do.'

Afterwards Hugh drove us back to his house for a drink. He lived in Brooklyn, and at first the district resembled some of the streets in the Village, but when Hugh turned into the street where he lived, it was as if we had driven into the set of a period movie – New York *circa* 1930. Kate gave a little gasp of pleasure and surprise. The cast-iron lamp-posts were freshly and lovingly repainted, the surface of the street was smoothly cobbled and the pavement was dotted with small flowering trees. Half-way down another tree rose out of the cobbles, its branches arching towards the brownstones on both sides. The street was clean and elegant, like a beautifully restored vintage automobile.

'This is what I call urban regeneration, man,' Kate said.

Hugh nodded, with an air that was both proud and somehow bashful. 'The block committee had the idea of making it look like old Brooklyn. The people in the street put a lot of work into it.'

The inside of Hugh's house was even more beautiful. A curving staircase climbed up from the black and white tiles in the hall to a huge, round skylight made of rose-coloured glass. The room we sat in was large and comfortable, with French windows which looked out on to a garden. It was a proper garden, not an American backyard, with a riot of ferns and flowers, a lily pond and a small greenhouse in one corner.

'Some garden,' Kate said.

'Well,' Hugh said. 'A tree grows in Brooklyn pretty good.'

Jane had greeted us like old friends. She poured whisky generously, and we settled down for a talk about our afternoon in the South Bronx. In what seemed like a short while I began to feel the effect of the drink.

'How did you two meet?' Jane asked suddenly.

Kate told her briefly. 'It must be expensive flying back and forth,' Jane said. She laughed. 'There's got to be problems.'

For a moment I thought Kate would say something sharp, but at that point there was a clatter on the stairs and their daughter Helen came into the room. She was a poised, polite fifteen-year-old with only a hint of cheekiness to suggest her age. She was going to stay the night with a friend and there was some mild wrangling with Jane about when she should come back. After she left the evening passed pleasantly, and by the time we got back to the Village we were too drowsy and too drunk to do more than pick up a pizza and tumble into bed.

We got back to Boston early, and Kate went straight in to the University. I went back to the apartment to prepare my lecture. By the late afternoon I had watched three quiz shows on TV, read a Robert Parker thriller set in Boston and rounded it off by seeing two old movies and a soap opera.

At six o'clock I was walking up the stairs of the research group's building. A two-storeyed, wooden colonial house set in its own grounds, it was big enough for a large family, and it belonged exclusively to the twenty or so members of the group. Most of them were already there, working their way through the light buffet that was laid out on the table in the hall. Kate, who had been waiting for me, made introductions, which I acknowledged in something of a daze. Some of the people I already knew, and I recognized most of them as types I was familiar with – assistant professors and PhD students. There was, however, a group of half a dozen older men and women who looked like department heads, real honest-to-goodness professors. Kate's historian was one of them.

'He looks like a mean asshole,' I muttered to Kate, but she merely squeezed my hand and winked.

In the event my apprehension was excessive. I had forgotten that even the historians and students of English politics would have had little knowledge about contemporary trends and developments apart from newspaper reports. The word 'anecdotal' was more or less a term of abuse among my own colleagues in England, but it wasn't long after I'd begin my lecture that I realized this group was interested precisely in the anecdotes which communicated the sound and feel of political life. I had started out describing the phenomenon of the bed-sitter politician and the strains appearing between Labour's machine politicians, the unions and the constituencies. I went on to describe the claims for a new electoral coalition among the GLC and the other Labour-dominated metropolitan councils. Confidence growing, I drew short sketches of politicians like Ken Livingstone and Paul Boateng. By now I was in full flow. I was coming over well, and I could see Kate at the back of the room nodding and smiling at me. I stopped after an hour, and the audience began asking questions, which merely required more descriptive detail. I was happy to oblige. An argument about trade unionism broke out between the historian and a research student,

and I sat back and let them wrangle. In a flash it was all over. Afterwards the historian came up and shook my hand. He gave me a small
smile and said he'd enjoyed my talk. Kate, who was standing beside
me, poked me in the back as he left, and muttered, 'one small step
for man.'

We ended the evening in a Chinese restaurant nearby, with about
a dozen people who'd attended the lecture. I knew only a few of them
but I was in no mood to quibble. I was in a euphoric mood which
seemed to be matched by the rest of the little group. This, Harvard
Square, was their stamping ground, where they could, and were
expected to, let off steam. So, warmed by alcohol and stimulated by
political argument, we roared and laughed and shouted.

I was struck, once again, by the contrast between what I knew
about these people and the sheer violence of their language. They
used words like horse's ass, fuck, shit, asshole, as terms of mild
emphasis. Opponents would be wiped out and blown away. Until
one got used to it, the frequency with which they used such language
seemed incongruous for such highly educated and thoughtful
people.

We occupied a large round table in the middle of the restaurant,
and Kate, sitting opposite, was so far away that I had to shout to
speak to her. Next to me sat Maria, one of her colleagues and a close
friend. Suddenly, half-way between the Peking dumplings and the
spare-ribs, Maria, a short, fierce, buxom woman in her thirties,
gripped my knee and spoke quietly.

'Do you love her?'

'What?' I said, confused.

'I asked you if you loved her,' she repeated impatiently. I was silent
for a moment. The question, in that place and time, seemed aggres-
sively intimate.

'Don't give me that goddam British reserve,' she yelled suddenly,
loud enough to be heard by everyone.

'I'm not,' I said, feeling stupid and defensive.

'Leave him alone,' Kate shouted from the other side of the table.

'You leave us alone,' Maria shouted back. 'We're doing fine.'

'Yes,' I whispered frantically. I didn't know how serious Maria was. The intimacy between Kate and her closest friends, and the intense loyalty they cultivated made me feel wary. 'I do. I do,' I muttered.

Maria rose a little from her seat.

'He loves you,' she announced to the table. Everyone laughed and applauded.

'Of course he does,' Kate said calmly. 'You think he's crazy?'

Before I could reply, the woman sitting on the other side of me asked a question about the Brixton riot. 'Is it true they call it an uprising?' she said. I sighed internally but it gave me a good excuse to turn away from Maria. Across the table Kate watched me with an oddly quizzical expression, and I made a mental note to ask her about the incident. But by the end of the evening I was too drunk and elated to remember.

The following day I was due to go to New York to give the lectures for which Hugh had engaged me. Before I left, however, I was to address a class of Kate's. This was an easy assignment, since it was a small class, and, in any case, only half its members had turned up for the lecture. One black boy kept falling asleep. At first I glanced at him repeatedly, but no one else remarked on it, and after a while I took no notice. Later on, over a cup of coffee, I asked about this boy.

'He's the brightest in the class,' she said. 'But he's got a regular job at night. It's the only way he can afford to be here. He turns up to everything but he gets tired.'

I was in New York by the late afternoon. I had expected to return in a couple of days, but a number of demands kept me occupied, so that it was nearly a week before I could get back to Boston.

The shuttle touched down in the late afternoon, and Kate met me as I emerged from the airport lounge. We stopped at the supermarket on the way home. We were entertaining that evening, she told me. A professor from Berkeley, who had taught her when she was there, would be in Boston, and she'd invited him for dinner. He was an old friend, but she also wanted to talk to him. The prospect depressed me slightly, because I had been hoping to put my feet up and watch TV, and I consoled myself with the thought that the old boy would probably leave early.

As it happened the professor was a surprise. He was short and balding but, far from being old, he seemed to be only a few years older than Kate, and he had an outrageously camp manner. 'England,' he said, one hand on his hip. 'England. I had a good time in England.'

'Sit down, Stanley,' Kate said. When he talked like this she treated him with a kind of amused tolerance, and he seemed to play up to it. Sitting down, he launched immediately into a story about being mugged a few days before, in a Los Angeles car-park.

'I arrived, sweetheart, just as they had finished taking off the tyres, and they looked at me as if I'd interrupted them in the middle of the workday. Well, don't let me stop you, dears, I thought. But before I could back out this guy stuck a knife half-way up my left nostril. Oh my God.' We made suitable noises of horror. 'Los Angeles is finished,' he concluded, 'and San Francisco isn't what it was. The sooner the earthquake takes us all off the better.'

'A friend of ours wants to go there,' Kate remarked casually. She went on to tell him about Alvarez and Maria, as I thought she would, sooner or later. He had read their work and immediately said he could get them part-time work in the sociology department. There were always, he thought, a few favours he could call in. Talking about these prospects and about the politics of the university, he sounded shrewd and capable, and it struck me that he might have been putting on a camp act for my benefit.

'Of course,' he said reflectively, 'anything more permanent might be impossible. It's not a good time for people on the Left to be looking for jobs, even in crazy California.'

'It's not so good here either,' Kate told him. 'A year ago if you were part of the left-wing caucus you were in. Nowadays I'm a little worried it might damage my chances.'

He looked at her consideringly. 'I don't think so.'

He had been meeting some of the university hierarchy, and, as his old pupil, Kate's name might have come up.

'Have you heard anything?' she asked him directly.

He shrugged. 'Nothing bad.' He paused. 'Of course, if you wanted to come to the coast, sweetheart, we could find you something.'

'I'll wait till I hear the offer.' She laughed. 'I'd be looking for something good.'

'Things could change,' he said. 'The Left is under heavy pressure, especially since the arrests.'

Kate nodded. 'I think they'll be making raids all over during the next few weeks.'

For a moment I couldn't understand what they were talking about, then I made the connection. While I was in New York, an armed gang had been arrested in the act of hijacking a payroll delivery. They had shot and killed the two guards and had been caught making their get-away. They were led by a woman who was a radical figure of the late 1960s. A member of the Weathermen, she dropped out of university and went underground. At one point she was on the FBI's list of most wanted criminals, and during the previous decade she had popped up again and again, as the mastermind of 'revolutionary' bombings and the instigator of a number of armed robberies. Her arrest had been a shock to a number of people, especially those who had been active in the 1960s and could remember the Weathermen, the Vietnam demos and the sense of solidarity which had linked students and young people in opposition to the machine of government and society. This woman had been the last relic of those times, and in the newspaper photos she had looked sad and lost and defiant all at the same time.

'I don't think these people had anything to do with what's going on now,' I said.

'They don't,' Kate replied. 'But the FBI's bound to use it as an excuse to crack down on some people.'

'And generally,' Stanley joined in, 'the Right can use it as propaganda against liberal attitudes.'

'That's right,' Kate said. 'They'll have a show trial where they'll drag out a lot of stuff, they'll raid every liberal organization they can think of and try and connect her to them, and they'll stir it all up into a justification for the Right. It's already happening, the way they use the notion of terrorism as some sort of creeping threat. The kids in my classes keep on asking me about terrorism because the only mention of politics they hear on TV or read in the papers is linked with terrorism.' She was in full flight now, and she got up and walked around the table. 'Some genius proposed to me the other day that we should run a course about the roots of terrorism, starting with Marx. And they've got this fashion for adding an "ic" to the end of words to give it a nasty ideological tinge. Terroristic. Communistic. Idealistic. Assholes.'

'The tragedy is,' Stanley said, 'that all those kids who went underground did it out of pure idealism.'

The trial was to be held in a small town where the shootings had taken place, and the townspeople would provide, according to Stanley, 'a hanging jury'. His tone was sentimental and he spoke about the gang as if they were martyrs.

'They're not exactly martyrs,' I said sharply. 'They blew away two middle-aged men who were merely driving along thinking about getting home to their families. I don't call that a blow against the system, and I don't see why it has anything to do with the Left or with the practice of politics, or why you're sitting here defending them.'

'You don't understand,' Stanley replied. He was holding himself in check and maintaining a reasonable tone, but I could see that my interjection had shocked both him and Kate. 'I knew them all.' He mentioned some of the underground people. 'They were all nice kids who thought they had no option. You've got to remember the atmosphere of the time. They saw themselves as being forced into it.'

'So did the James gang, and Bonnie and Clyde,' I said. 'It seems to me that they had themselves a ball. Shooting, robbery, blowing things up, all in the name of revolution. If all goes to plan, they'll be out in a few years, running ad agencies.'

By now the atmosphere in the kitchen was rather chilly, but we all remained more or less polite, and it wasn't long before Stanley said he had a meeting in the morning and had to go. Kate came back from seeing him out in an angry mood, as I could tell by the vigour with which she washed up and put things back in their places.

'Maybe I was a bit heavy,' I said to her. 'But I just couldn't stand the way he was sitting there dripping sympathy for these creeps whose only proof of their idealism was to kill a few bank guards. One of them was a poor old black man just about to retire. I can just see that turning on the oppressed classes.'

'Would it make things any better,' she replied, 'if he had been a member of the Klan?'

'At least,' I said, 'it would have been a move in the right direction.'

'All right. You identify with the black guard who got himself killed. You must be able to see why Stanley identifies with the underground.'

'No, I can't,' I said. 'I can understand that they've got the same background but I can't understand him defending the violence. I could understand it if he was different. But the man's a frightened rabbit. He wouldn't do it himself and he's terrified of violence. I could tell when we started arguing. If I'd lifted my hand to him he would have got under the table. And this is the guy who's sitting in the stands clapping when the underground blows away another citizen.'

'I knew it,' Kate shouted. 'I knew it. You were uncomfortable from the moment he came in, and you saw he was gay. You're just telling me that you're more macho than he is. Big deal.'

For a moment I almost acknowledged the truth of what she'd said. But that was only a very small part of it. My irritation was directed at both Kate and Stanley because their concern was so narrow. Several of the surviving underground people had already been captured or given themselves up. Some had served short prison sentences, some had been given immunity in return for their evidence. Most of them, coming as they did from prosperous families, had been well represented in court, and afterwards had found themselves good jobs or made money from the sale of their memoirs. In comparison with the average petty criminal they had done well. One of them, interviewed in the *New York Times*, had become an advertising executive. Many of my black friends in New York and London spent half a lifetime working doggedly to get jobs on the same level. For all I knew there were numbers of whites in the same position. The underground people got the best of all worlds. It was as if nothing could go wrong for them, no matter how hard they tried, and it was galling to hear them being talked of as idealistic martyrs.

'It's nothing to do with him being gay,' I said. 'It's these people roaming through the world with their guns and their unshakeable conviction that they're entitled to shoot or bomb anyone because they happen to disagree with the government. They're not even fanatics, they're just spoiled, self-indulgent kids.'

'They're not like that at all.' She mentioned the leader of the gang, the one whose face had been staring out of the front pages. 'She's not like that at all. You'd like her if you met her.' She was watching me slyly.

'The hell I would,' I said.

'Got you,' she cried out triumphantly. 'You did meet her and you did like her. You said she was sexy. You spent half the night talking to her, and you'd probably have brought her back here if I'd let you.'

For the moment I couldn't work out what she meant, and then I realized she was talking about one of the women who had been at the table on the night we went to the Chinese restaurant. She had been tall, with short brown hair and warm, smiling eyes. It was she who had asked me about the black community in Britain. I would have remembered her in any case, if only because she was so quiet and softly spoken in comparison with the rest of the group.

'I can't believe it,' I said. Even while I was taking this in, however, it struck me that Kate, like half the people at the table that night, had been at Berkeley at the same time as some of the underground people. These had been her friends and fellow activists. 'Why didn't you tell me?' I asked her.

'What was the point? What would you have done?'

I didn't know the answer to that. 'Weren't you scared the police would walk in or something?'

She shrugged. 'The pictures they had of her were more than ten years old. It was years since anyone recognized her. Anyway, no one had been in touch with her for years. She just turned up. We could hardly throw her out.'

'She must have been planning the robbery then,' I said slowly. It seemed incredible.

'I suppose she was,' Kate replied.

'It's unbelievable,' I repeated.

'I know,' Kate said. 'She was such a nice kid.'

— 10 —

Black British Writing –
So What Is It?

In Britain, the concept of blackness with which most of us are obliged
to work at the moment has been constructed since the post-war wave
of immigration. It has roots in the experience of the Civil Rights
struggle in the USA. It derives partly from the rhetoric of pan-
Africanism which was born in the Caribbean and amplified in one
period of African history – the period associated with decolonization
in Ghana. Its most important contemporary resonances spring from
its use in black popular music over the last couple of decades, so
we're stuck with a notion which has been partly constructed in
Britain, but not for Britain, and not solely or necessarily by black
people.

In recent years commercial needs have even begun to dictate the
use of the term. For instance, blackness is the trip-wire for a number
of cues in television advertising or pop music videos, and we're now
so saturated with an imagery which screams 'blackness' that the
term itself is often emptied of meaning and becomes a simple repetition of bits of played out polemic or the framework for advertising
slogans. The irony is that black writing in Britain may be standing at
the gateway to a subject matter which informs a number of what will
be crucial global issues for this new century. The relationship
between nationalism, ethnicity, nationality and citizenship, for
example, or between poverty and wealth, between reality and myth
and between different kinds of conflicting identities, both public and
private.

Black writers, whether we like it or not, begin by being deeply
engaged in these matters, because they are part of our daily experi-

ence and part of how we have to construct our own lives. Nevertheless, we work within an environment shaped by a routine and rigidly limited expectation of our capacity to engage with such issues. As a result, the first response of most readers in Britain to the title of this chapter is likely to be a reprise of the question: what is black British writing anyway?

At one level the answer is that black writing is what black writers do, and that's a tempting formulation because once analysis and description begins, the whole notion begins to escape from both the writer and the reader and takes on the shape of a theoretical maze. But this is an old-fashioned narrative, and you can rely on what I'm saying. In spite of the dangers it is still important, in a number of different ways, to explore the question: in Britain, what does black writing mean?

A characteristic difficulty is confusion over labels already validated by the conventions attached to race and skin colour. Over the past two decades critics and academics have invented a category to describe the work of writers from territories which were once colonies, and outside the USA every writer of African descent has had his or her work labelled 'postcolonial' by the gurus of contemporary criticism. 'Blackness' is usually bracketed in this category, and there's a neat continuity implied there, so it is necessary to probe what lies behind these terms before it becomes possible to see what black writing in Britain is about.

Black immigrants from Africa and the Caribbean left behind societies and cultures which were in various different stages of crisis. In Britain during much of the twentieth century, a black person was generally presumed to be a native of somewhere else – an alien. But the literatures which had begun to invent themselves in Africa and the Caribbean derived from a tradition which any English speaker could recognize. Such Caribbean writers as Reid, Mais, Selvon, Lamming and Naipaul began with the same models which were used by any English writer, as did African writers like Chinua Achebe and Ngugi.

Nevertheless, the resemblances were deceptive. In the period when the great experience of decolonization was taking place,

African and Caribbean writers were adopting very different attitudes to the business of constructing a national identity. African writers were beginning to draw on the sources available to them in the myths and languages of their region. It is significant, for instance, that a writer like James Ngugi moved from the use of English to the use of an African language and from being plain James Ngugi to the name Ngugi Wa Thiongo. This wasn't an inward movement that was available to Caribbean writers, and after the 1950s English-speaking Caribbean writers were moving in another direction, namely outwards. Unlike most other regions the Caribbean didn't have an economy which could sustain writers, and even if the region could have done so, most of the important Caribbean writers would still have felt the need to join the huge decanting of people which was emigration. So if you name a Caribbean writer you're also naming someone who is likely to be teaching in an American or Canadian university. There's another element to Caribbean writing which is frequently dismissed or overlooked but which has an important effect in its history. The societies of the Caribbean were by and large multiracial assemblies in which the notion of blackness had been deeply ambiguous and hotly contested. Edgar Mittelholzer, for instance, in his Kaywana novels about a family in Guyana, draws up a completely racist map of identity. His world view parallels the doctrines of the Nazis, and in it the whites are superior, the black people are close to animals and the mixture of the races leads to madness and chaos. He also believed himself to be a pure-blooded descendant of Swiss settlers and looked back to the racist ethic of slavery with nostalgia. He was an authentic Guyanese, none more so, and he killed himself, using a bundle of fireworks on Hampstead Heath.

V. S. Naipaul, who was born in Trinidad, animates the Indian caste system to claim Brahmin ancestry, and his books describe a kind of cultural caste system in which black Africans occupy the lowest rung of the ladder. One of the best is entitled *The Mimic Men*, which is a fair description of how the book sets out the relationship of the Caribbeans to the civilization of the world.

The Caribbean provenance of these writers can't be ignored or dismissed, because their beliefs are in fact deeply embedded in the culture of the region, which illustrates the danger of assuming that Caribbean writing is, by definition, 'black' writing. It is also an illustration of the problem faced by black writers in almost any segment of the African diaspora. For most readers, critics and sometimes writers themselves, in a context dominated by the imagery of African-American identity, it has become a reflex to subsume the local and regional distinctiveness of black writers within a universalized rhetoric of 'blackness'.

The postcolonial label creates similar problems which can be illustrated by a cursory sketch of what's happening in the work of African and Caribbean writers. In the African tradition, decolonization permitted the emergence of a group of writers who could pull together and reflect a number of narratives and philosophical attitudes which are deeply grooved in the life of communities around them and clearly transmitted through the languages and the history. The Yoruba tradition, for instance, influences a line of writers from Amos Tutuola to Ben Okri. The other influence which shaped African writing was the engagement of writers, animated by the critical state of politics and society in the societies they came from. Wole Soyinka, Ngugi, Achebe and a raft of writers in southern Africa are typical examples of how this confrontation focused the writers' concern on the moral and ethical issues of a rapidly changing environment.

There is a very different picture in the Caribbean, or to be more precise, out of the Caribbean. The most important Caribbean writers – Lamming, Wilson Harris, Salkey and Walcott – became names honoured in the region. At the same time, all their work reflects the sheer porousness and ambiguity of Caribbean identity. The grand narrative of the Caribbean is a narrative about engagement with the world outside the region, and if there is a tradition which frames the writing of the Caribbean, it is the tradition of dispersal. Nevertheless, the concept – 'blackness' – was a crucial part of the influences which, in these regions, liberated generations of writers to explore their own identity and traditions.

In comparison, the narrative animating black British writers is rooted in an awareness of what it meant to leave Africa or the Caribbean or Asia, and to enter the industrialized world of Europe.

It was in this context that the Africans and Caribbeans who came to live here became black, but timing is everything, and by the time we began writing about our transformed identity a series of endlessly deceptive models had already been imposed on our experience. The problem is not so much to do with blackness as such. In different circumstances it would be possible to put our blackness in perspective. White writers are hardly distracted by their whiteness, since for them, its practical consequences are trivial. On the other hand, black writers in Britain live in an environment where it's taken for granted that their identity is defined and limited by the colour of their skins. At the same time, although black people have an undeniable historical presence in Britain, their absence from the image of the nation's culture is equally undeniable. When they say 'black writing', most people in Britain are referring either to the skin colour of the author or to a bundle of characteristics associated with the Caribbean, Africa and black America.

In the USA, however, black writing signals a chronological outline of African-American life stretching back to slavery and highlighting some of the most important moments in the nation's history. In comparison, black British writing has little presence and no hinterland in the imagination of our publics. Partly as a result, black writers in Britain have always been faced with the implicit requirement of reproducing the style and content of a black canon which was shaped and conceived in circumstances of which they have no experience and with which they have little empathy.

The problem is a relatively recent one. During the 1950s and 1960s, when Caribbean migration to Britain was at its height, writers came to Britain from the West Indies in order to publish and to kickstart the idea of a Caribbean literature into existence. On the other side of the coin British academics and publishers like Heinemann were cultivating African writers and nurturing the birth of an African literature. Few, if any, of the black writers operating in Britain at that time were concerned with conditions in Britain or with what it meant to grow up and live in the United Kingdom. Equally, the concept of 'blackness' which permeated the consciousness of our world was that which had been created within the crucible of the struggle for

Civil Rights in the USA. In comparison, the experience of black people who had grown up in Britain, and felt they belonged there, was, in literary terms, more or less invisible.

Over the past fifty years this has been a situation which precisely matched the prejudices of the British book trade, along with its academic and literary counterparts. With a few significant exceptions, these institutions have maintained a tradition of treating black people as aliens, outsiders to the body of British society. The ruling literary circles in Britain therefore had no difficulty in honouring Caribbean, African and black American writers, or in studying the texts written by such authors, as long as they could be conveniently distanced from the practice of native English writing. Publishers followed suit, and for a long time it was easier for a black writer living in the Commonwealth to be published in Britain than for a black person born and brought up in London or Birmingham.

Black artists and writers who had developed in Britain, or claimed their British environment as a legitimate subject, tended to be ghettoized and segregated into the smallest cultural space available; and given the fact that the key to success depended on the extent to which black artists could impersonate 'alien' voices, the content and style of much of the work we produced had to be derivative or frank imitations of foreign successes.

Until recently, this was a context which actively discouraged black writers from developing domestic subjects. To be worthy of the glittering prizes of literature black writers seemed obliged to impose on themselves a distance of time, geography or sympathy.

The situation has been partly a consequence of our relationship with audiences. Who were we addressing when we wrote our stories? At one level the answer is easy – anyone who cares to read them. But the structure of the trade dictates otherwise. In practice our readers are usually white people. This doesn't mean that 'black people don't read', as more than one bookseller has told me. Of course they read, but what they read and how they get to it is a complex and embattled matter. Black people read road signs, and official letters and computer screens and newspapers. You can see them doing it any time and anywhere you care to look. When it comes to fiction, history or biography, however, the system of marketing, distribution and delivery drives an effective wedge between black writers and black audiences. In these circumstances black writers in Britain are likely to be struggling with a species of domestic exile which widens the gap between themselves and their own experience. But this isn't simply a problem for the writers. There's another dimension. Look at history and follow the money. The pioneering entrepreneurs of the black community in this country didn't even have to think about the routes along which their enterprises led them. The niches were ready-made for black beauty products, cheap travel to the Caribbean or Africa, and the import of tropical foods. All these provided a series of stepping-stones for a natural expansion of a market which could support a variety of other products. The foundations of black women's magazines are to be found as much in this tradition as in imitation of their white competitors. These were the exceptions which proved the rule. In general, the big bucks came from those commodities which tended to be controlled by white multinational corporations.

Ask a cross-section of black people what books they read, and the answer you'll get is a broad variety: John Grisham, Thomas Harris, Alice Walker, Toni Morrison, various self-help manuals, and even the Bible. They suit themselves, picking and mixing from a wide variety of trends and influences. So the first hurdle for black British writers has been both the relative lack of power and the fragmented nature of the only group which could have demanded the assembly of a coherent narrative about the experience of black people in Britain.

In the absence of a dominant narrative, writers tackling the problem of black identity in Britain have tended to be thrown back on a universalized concept of 'blackness', which is a complex, tangled notion if you happen to be British, no matter what the colour of your skin.

Is the blackness of an asylum seeker from Angola, for instance, the same as the blackness of a light-skinned part-African Caribbean? Or a part-Indian, part-European from Goa? Are Asians really black, even if some of them reject the label with contempt?

The available ideas about the colour of our skins and our

relationship to it didn't help in resolving such problems. Almost all the black writing which we could use as models came out of a background which was relatively homogeneous. The exceptions were troubling. Samuel Selvon, for instance, one of the few Caribbeans who had written about the city with any impact, had turned black people in London into comic caricatures or sentimentalized victims. At the other end of the scale black writers were confronted by a tradition of English writing in which they were absent, or contemptuously relegated to a role which defined the outer limits of whiteness.

Equally, our vocation was informed by a new ethos which forced a virtual imprisonment within the idea of race and blackness. This was multiculturalism, which, during the late 1970s and 1980s, became a euphemism for the assembly of races in London and the larger cities. Whatever else multiculturalism was, it had also become a doctrine which provided an escape route from the implications of racial equality. Within the funding and conduct of the arts, the ruling councils invented roles for the 'alien cultures' which suggested that they were regarded as the equal of the 'mainstream'. In practice this meant that blacks and Asians were funded and supported in organizing separate cultural artefacts, which soaked up their oppositional energies. The theory and practice of multiculturalism could therefore only be justified by the production of a stream of images which offered a clear and unambiguous delineation of black otherness.

So the policy of bodies like the British Council and the Arts Council towards our writing developed in tandem with an academic criticism which either ignored the black British or tacked us on as a footnote to a body of 'postcolonial' work largely dominated by Asians and Africans. Within this burgeoning market theoretical arguments about migrant identity in Britain tended to be based on the anachronistic reading of 'postcolonial' texts, written two or three decades ago, as if they were the product of contemporary conditions. Equally, recent texts tend to be read as if they had emerged from an earlier and rather different 'postcolonial' environment.

It was clear that the psychological consequences of colonialism continued to have implications for the discussion of nationality and identity. On the other hand, the psychoanalytical speculations which Franz Fanon had taken from his colonial experience half a century before had been enshrined by a generation of theorists as fixed and eternal truths about the identity of black people everywhere. The result was to imprison our attempts to explore nationality and identity within a deterministic view of ethnicity. For a time this was a dominant ethos which locked the imagination of black writers in Britain into the framework of race and racism, and reinforced the tradition in which black writing was to be viewed as merely another step in our universal confrontation with whiteness, irrespective of where and why it was taking place.

In the circumstances, the environment in which we were to launch our efforts tended to categorize us as primers to the essential nature of blacks. On the other side of the coin, the only imagery we could draw on had already been described for us by the traditions of our common culture, and prescribed an endless repetition of its clichés. Even the critics who labelled our work assumed that we were merely younger versions of the Caribbean or African writers who had passed through Britain as students, and for whom the experience was a transient stage in their development.

This was the landscape facing me when I set out to write my first novel. The first decision I made was that it would be located in a specific genre. I wanted to write about London, and I wanted to write about it in my voice rather than in the voice of a white Englishman or a foreign 'postcolonial'. To achieve this I had both to confront English literary traditions and throw off the universalized imagery and generalized concerns of blackness which I felt like a dead weight on my shoulders. The narrative and formal discipline of a genre, I decided, would be my escape route. I chose crime fiction by reflex, but when I started thinking about how to do it a number of problems emerged.

I had assumed that all I needed to do was to reproduce the conventions of the genre, substituting my own black persona for that of a white man. But halfway through my first page I started to feel uneasy, and it wasn't long before my uneasiness developed into the conviction that the conventions I was trying to reproduce were also a polemical statement about the nature of society.

I found out later that writers in the genre like to argue about differing shades of realism, but the truth is that reality has nothing to do with it. Instead, the routine fantasies of crime fiction have moulded popular imaginations, and most of us now perceive our everyday reality in the terms of a crime story – mean streets, lurking rapists and burglars, serial killers. Ask anyone who knows and they'll tell you that the fear of being mugged, burgled or murdered is the modern neurosis, out of all proportion to the actual chances of it happening.

Appropriately, true crime reports in the media echo the style of crime fiction, ironically demonstrating that real-life events now depend for their credibility on the style of a fictional narrative. The O. J. Simpson trial on TV, for example, was prefaced by a *film noir* title sequence and theme music. Egged on by the media, most people followed the case in the terms of a crime fiction, deciding early whodunit, and reacting with rage when the narrative reached the 'wrong' conclusion and the baddy got off. In the real world the story would have been about evidence, probability and the right of the defendant to the presumption of innocence. But the classic elements of the story – the beautiful blonde, the boyfriend, the possessive husband – had already closed the gap between fiction and reality, so from that point the rules of the genre dictated public responses. This is the essence of crime fiction, a struggle between goodies and baddies, which also tells you who the baddies are, what their social or racial background is and what part of town they live in.

Crime fiction also describes a moral world as static as the medieval universe, heaven on top and hell below. Baddies over there, goodies over here. But nowadays morality has unhooked itself from religion, and has become a matter of majority consensus – law and order. Crime fiction is a powerful influence in the shape and direction of this consensus, and the detectives have become its custodians and enforcers.

This was the point at which my identity as a black writer intersected the needs of the genre, and it was one of the reasons, I concluded later, that had drawn me to a tradition with which I was instinctively in conflict. A statement about history and nationality ran like an unbroken thread through British writing about crime, whether or not it was fiction. The focus is invariably an idealized outline of an imaginary paradise of unchallenged white nationalism. 'Warm beer and cricket on the village green' as an unspoken reference evokes a time when everyone knew their place, crime was isolated to the slum areas and uppity black men were dealt with as they deserved. This is the nastier side of the nostalgia for inept crossword merchants like Agatha Christie, but it also outlines the central vision of contemporary crime fiction. Run through the genre, from the other side of the Atlantic with writers like Elmore Leonard to recent British creations like *Cracker*, and what you see is the swelling paranoia of an embattled 'white' morality, surrounded and threatened by an irresistible tide of alien evil.

The statistics of crime and punishment illustrate the interaction of real life with this fictional imagery. In the USA African-Americans are 12 per cent of the population, but nearly 50 per cent of the prisoners. In Britain black men are 17 per cent more likely to be imprisoned than white men.

This is white power, a concrete statement about the nature of criminals and criminality, and it says that the outsider is the source and agent of crime, the snake in the Garden. To be black in this world of crime fiction morality is to be an irretrievable outsider. So for a black writer like myself, squaring the circle presented an opportunity to engage with an argument about British identity from outside the conventional framework of race thinking.

It was clear that I couldn't reproduce or even enter the grand narrative of my white colleagues, because my own identity put me firmly on the side of evil. Black writers before me had faced this hurdle. For example, Chester Himes, reputedly the doyen of black crime fiction, had created a world in which every conceivable issue was narrowed down to a confrontation between blacks and whites. In this world everyone was crippled and deformed by their obsession with race, and every relationship of every kind was determined by race. The author's surrogates were two black detectives, psychotics driven by a deep rage to beat and kill other blacks. It was, in its way, a mirror image of a white racist's universe, and a reworking of Himes's own internal conflicts, but his white readers felt they were descending into the moral underworld of black life, while at the same time confirming their prejudices about the social and moral hierarchy. Himes suffered intense frustration, and although he never managed to challenge the preconceptions of race in his fiction, he tried to atone by campaigning for North African rights in France.

Since then, several black writers had followed Himes's style of treating the exploration of his background as a descent into the moral underground, and they varied from a network of African-American narratives about gangster life, to the bungling drug-dealer chic of Yardies in Britain.

I already perceived Himes, however, as a dreadful object lesson about the seductive charisma of the role occupied by blacks in a racist view of the world. In comparison, I saw my characters as being charged with the regeneration of a moral wilderness that my fellow writers had kept at bay. Deliberately trying to sidestep the implications of a typical narrative about blackness, I based my first story on the Oedipus myth.

Drawing on the basic conventions of the genre, Sam Dean, the hero of my first book, *Blood Rights*, was a black freelance journalist regularly hired to sort out problems for white power brokers and the black perspective he brings to the situation challenges their moral certainties, but he is continually obliged to reconstitute his own moral code within a culture where he is a moral outlaw.

Publication confirmed my sense of isolation. Reviewers kept comparing me to Chester Himes and Raymond Chandler, firmly attaching me to both of the conventions I was trying to dodge. I had published my second book before I began discovering allies. Walt Mosley's first book, *Devil in a Blue Dress*, was set in 1948, challenging the white version of a historical moral utopia head-on, exploring the racial oppression and malice which surrounded the black communities in LA at the time.

Later on I read Barbara Neeley's *Blanche on the Lam*, whose heroine, a middle-aged black cleaning woman, gets a gaol sentence for passing bad cheques, goes on the lam, and when a dead body is discovered in her white employers' house, has to use a network of black cleaning women to locate the killer and clear herself of suspicion.

These, among others, were works which seemed, like mine, to be trying to take a world which functioned both inside and outside the framework of race as its location, presenting the black characters as ordinary human beings with a full range of human sympathies, and using the issue of crime as an instrument for exploring the immorality of various kinds of social exclusion.

The result is that readers who identify with their heroes have their universe turned upside-down. In the worlds of my migrant protagonists we were the goodies, and the real threat of the mean streets was the paranoia of the white world about our presence. Around us were conditions which, for our families and friends, have often slammed shut the avenues to economic survival, apart from petty crime. The real crimes were to do with cruelty, with physical and social confinement, with racial oppression and hatred. As my stories developed, an illuminating gap between black and white perceptions of crime and punishment emerged. In white crime fiction, being on the other side of the moral fence was a symptom of criminality and deviance. To me, it was the shape of real life.

Writing crime fiction had begun to demonstrate that I had a subject which didn't confine me within the colour of my skin, but which gave me a platform from which I could exploit my roots in the experience of being black in Britain, while linking my writing to themes which extended beyond race and location. In my own work I had been obliged to mount an argument about how people could transform themselves within various cultural sites, and about how swapping the beliefs and influences which shaped our lives challenged the power of ideology. In the process, what seemed to be emerging was a stubbornly unruly marketplace of cultures, ideas and people, where physical and psychological divisions continually shift and change.

It was this platform which during recent decades has begun to define and characterize black British writing. Given that its roots are in the black communities' attempts to describe and explore its own nature, it is a fairly recent phenomenon. In the past decade, however, a group of authors whose work features recognizable common elements have begun to emerge. They range from those who are widely acclaimed such as Caryl Phillips and Ben Okri, to the less well known like Nicola Williams. Their interests vary and so do the themes of their work. Some of them would resent being described as 'British', even though they might have been born or brought up exclusively in Britain. Almost all are eager to escape being confined within the attitudes to black writing which are conventional in Britain. On the other hand, it is possible to extract a few consistent strands which run through all of them, and which have begun to define the content of black British fiction.

First, there is a critical concern with identity and its relationship with a network of arguments about nationality and citizenship. This is accompanied by a focus on how the urban landscape shapes individual choices and outcomes, a consistent interest in excavating or describing the effects of migration on British society and a dominant interest in describing the language or motivation of black characters whose experience of growing up and living in Britain determines their identity.

These features, in one combination or the other, have begun to spearhead a new trend in contemporary English writing, although publishers and booksellers have been slow to grasp the point.

The issues which emerge will be crucial issues in the future of the twenty-first-century world – the relationship between nationalism, ethnicity, nationality and citizenship, between poverty and wealth, between reality and myth and between different kinds of conflicting identities, both public and private. These are the inevitable concerns of communities which are incoherent or fragmented, blurred at their edges, uncertain of their provenance at the centre, and incapable of controlling the manipulation of their identity. For the writers being thrown up by the experience of growing up and living in Britain, these are the concrete realities which are fundamental to the conduct of their lives outside of the printed page, and they constitute the building blocks of the black British narrative. If this is a movement, it is one which has been provoked and driven, through the limits outlined by race and racism, by the unique needs of the black British communities. This is the fact which has created and rescued black British writing, and finally makes it difficult to define in terms which fit traditional notions about blackness or Britishness, but, of course, that is precisely what it's all about.

— 11 —

The State of Fatherhood

My first child was born on a bright sunny morning in October 1974. I'd spent the previous twenty-four hours sitting in a waiting room at University College Hospital, so I'd had plenty of time to think. At about eleven o'clock a nurse came in and told me I had a son, and I rushed down the corridor, wanting to run, my only thought to see him. They were wheeling him out of the room in a cot, and I walked alongside, taking my first good look. He seemed impossibly little, battered and exhausted, a fighter at the end of a long struggle, his face bruised and marked by the forceps they'd used. We came to a door, and someone was trying to hurry me, pushing me out of the way, but I held on to the edge of the cot and stopped it going through for a moment. In that moment he opened his eyes and looked at me.

I remember that look even now. Dead level, something speculative about it, wondering. I've seen it many times since then, when he wants to tell me about something that's upset him, or when we're talking seriously and I've said something that puzzles or annoys him. It's a serious look which seems to come from the eyes I first saw so many years ago, when that straightforward questing stare was all there was to him, asking the same question: Like who's this guy?

A few minutes later I went out into the autumn sunshine, moving like a sleep-walker, automatically. I felt as if I was there and not there at the same time, as if the pavement, the buildings, the glitter of the sun on a windscreen, were products of my mind, insubstantial, unreal, and for a moment I couldn't figure out whether I was in the grip of some trauma brought on by the experience or whether I was just simply knackered.

I went round the corner to a café in Tottenham Court Road and bought a ham sandwich. I hadn't eaten since the previous morning and now I was starving. Walking back to the hospital I worried about the fact that, even though I'd been turning things over in my mind for the last couple of days, I hadn't come to any conclusions or made any decisions about what would happen or how we would live. At the time we lived in a bed-sitter in North London. I didn't have a job and there was nothing in sight. Freelancing and doing odd jobs brought in barely enough to pay the rent. From time to time during that morning I felt like a man setting out in a leaky rowing-boat to cross the Atlantic.

I can remember now that look my son gave me, but I can't remember thinking clearly about anything else during that period. What sticks in my mind is the fact that I had some idea of writing a diary about our life together, which just goes to show you what my mood was like – a kaleidoscope in which numbness gave way to fear which gave way to a crazy sentimentality.

Back in the waiting room I sat down and tried to begin writing my thoughts of the previous two days, but, as soon as I opened my notebook I realized that all I could recall was a jumble of memories and impressions. Struggling desperately to get a fix on my feelings I began scribbling a few sentences. *My son was born this morning*, I wrote. *He opened his eyes and looked at me. Now I know what love is.*

After that I closed the book, and I never wrote anything else in it. It's still in my possession, and occasionally, tidying up, I run across it, the covers neat and clean, three sentences stark against the empty pages.

There was never any question in my mind at any time during my life about whether or not I was going to be a father. I knew it was going to happen. I knew, also, that it was something to do with the logic of being a man. In the culture of the place and time where I was born, 'father' was a simple biological description. I knew kids whose fathers denied their existence. I knew kids whose fathers hardly spoke except when they hit them. I knew kids who had not seen their fathers for years. Later on I knew men whose adolescence had been spent in a battle of wills with their fathers. But, at the time, none of this made a dent in the concept of the thing. If you were lucky, your father looked after you with kindness and concern. But even if he was a bad father, no one else would do. The notion of 'fathering' was beside the point. In those circumstances contemporary buzz-words like nurture and caring were unknown, and, if they had been, would have made no sense. A father was the man whose potency had charged you with the spark of life, and so fatherhood and manhood were inextricably linked.

There was something about the very word that was electric, mystical, redolent of sacral power – God the Father. Fathers had the power to bless, the strength to protect and when you got right down to the wire, they could condemn, punish, cast you into the outer darkness. The Church certainly knew what it was doing when it gave its priests the title 'Father'.

I had precisely this sense of awe about my own father while he was alive, and my first clear memory of him contains a blend of worship, fear, shame and guilt which brings him back to me immediately, sharp and clearly present, the way I encounter him in my dreams. On this occasion I was still very young, about three years old, I suppose, and I was playing about in a pile of junk under our house, when I heard my father shouting my name. I was crouching out of sight inside an old cupboard and instead of answering I stayed hidden. Looking back, I don't know why I didn't answer right away. I suppose it must have been a combination of fear and mischief, but the longer he called, his voice sounding louder and more furious, the more difficult it became to come out of hiding. Even when the rest of the family joined in, a chorus of voices, I still didn't move. After a while they seemed to give up looking for me and things went quiet, so I crawled out to take a look. Everyone was clustered around the gate and I was just in time to see my father, dressed in his soldier's uniform, standing in the back of a lorry which was speeding off down the road. I understood immediately. While I'd been hiding from him, he'd been calling me to say goodbye. I started to run after the lorry, to try and catch him to say I was sorry, but it was too late. He didn't come back for a long time.

He died in the year my first son was born. I still dream about him, a tall young man, younger than I am now, and I watch him cautiously, wondering what he thinks about me, wanting to tell him many things. One time I rang my mum to tell her, and she said: He's trying to tell you something. Well, I'd figured that much out for myself, I told her, I just wish I knew what he was trying to say.

Sometimes I get a message from him, through the medium of my own feelings, a faint echo, which is a blend of memory and emotion. During our first years in England the cinema was my passion. I was one of only two black boys at my school, and it was a long time before I found a circle of friends. Sitting alone in the dark absorbed in the hypnotic flicker of the screen seemed natural and inevitable. Sometimes I'd sit there until they played the National Anthem, nerving myself up for the dash home, because, late at night, the streets of Hackney were still dangerous territory for a black teenager. At the top of our road I'd see my dad standing under a lamp-post. When he saw me coming he'd turn and go back into the house. In my head I still carry this image of him, standing up straight, steady as a rock in that circle of smoky light, peering through the darkness, trying to catch a glimpse of me.

When my first son was only a baby, a perfect little man, lying still and beautiful in his cot, I would have a recurring nightmare. We'd be out somewhere, and I'd turn around and find him gone, or suddenly I'd be miles away from where I'd left the pram, or I'd be holding him, running the gauntlet of angry crowds, faces contorted, hands and weapons lashing out at him. Waking up, I would go and take a look in his room, make sure he was all right. Sometimes, in the early hours of the morning, I'd be sitting at my desk writing, trying to find the right words, and I'd hear a sound behind me. When I turned around he'd be there, gazing at me, clutching his little blue blanket to his chest.

What I didn't know then, in the middle of my anxiety, was that this would be the easiest bit. Some varieties of parenting are easier, less complicated than others, and there are special difficulties about being a black father in a society like ours. Take these pointers, for instance. In my son's run-up to his GCSE exams I attended the year's first open day, where one of the teachers whom we encountered was a well-intentioned young man, who gave me a brief and well-rehearsed lecture about the importance of having books in the home and encouraging my son to read. By this time I was a university lecturer, a published author, and my own teaching career must have begun while the teacher in front of me was still in the cradle. My son had been playing with books before he could walk, and reading before he went near a school. But this particular teacher had no way of knowing this, and, I suppose, he had no way of knowing how patronizing his remarks were. What he saw in front of him was a black man, and that gave him his cue.

Another time, about nine in the morning, my son had just set out on some errand when I heard the doorbell ring. Thinking he'd forgotten his keys I opened the door to see him standing beside a policeman who had stopped him a few feet away from the front door and insisted on checking that he lived in the house from which he'd just emerged. This was Holland Park, but the policeman, new on the beat, was barely polite, and once I'd reassured him about my son, he turned his attention to me. 'How long have you been living here, sir?' was his next question.

In normal circumstances families have a sort of contract with the society in which they exist. The bargain is that you protect your children, and induct them into the conventions which govern our lives. In return you get an assurance of safety, and the promise of access to a range of services and opportunities. In practice life is unpredictable, because that's how things are, but, small print aside, most parents believe in this guarantee. Generally, fathers inherit a sense that they have a crucial public role to play in this process, which is precisely the background of feeling that gives a sharp edge to some of the current debates about parenting.

In this context, black men in our society have had to live with a continuing sense of being under attack. All of us have our prospects determined or limited by discrimination. Catch-22. Keep your head down, stay out of trouble and soldier through the routine of giving your family some sort of security, and you get typecast as a passive object of attitudes and conditions against which any man of spirit would rebel. If you take chances, pursue your ambitions and then fail, it qualifies you as an exemplar of the irresponsibility and inadequacy of your generation of black fathers. You can't win because, either way, the problems your children encounter will, sooner or later, be laid at your door, by a slew of experts and gurus in the classroom, or on TV, radio, in newspapers, and through every other medium available.

Shortly after my first son was born I began to experience new and curious feelings. I don't mean the sort of sentiment you feel while sitting and holding your child, poring over the sheer marvel of having produced this tiny, perfect creature. I expected that. This was something different, a cultural thing, I would have to call it, and the unexpected quality of my emotion was probably due to the way I'd begun to think about 'culture'. This was different to the ideas about culture with which I'd grown up. As a young immigrant I understood that we – that is, people from the country where I was born – were marked out and linked together by our customs: our food, our music, the dialect we spoke. We were accustomed to the idea that people from our region had always travelled far afield in search of work and better prospects. Sometimes they came back with the strangest customs and habits, but that made no difference, because you could live at the North Pole and eat whalemeat, or wear a grass skirt or learn to speak Chinese without ceasing to be one of us. We weren't proud of our lives, but we weren't ashamed either. Such things were only the decor of one's life. The culture was what we were inside, the way we felt about each other and about the world.

A couple of decades later, by the time my son was born, the culture to which I was supposed to belong had become 'black culture', and every time you heard the word it meant someone was trying to sell you something – a record, a ticket, membership of some group or allegiance to some campaign they had going. 'Our culture' was the phrase used by the dickhead who argued that I ought to plait my son's hair in dreadlocks, even though I had grown up having my head scraped to the scalp every fortnight under a mango tree, my father watching the barber sternly. 'Cut it clean,' he'd say. 'Your culture' was the phrase the teacher uttered when she read a poem written in the Barbadian dialect to my son's class, using what she imagined was a Jamaican accent, not knowing that the difference altered the feel and the meaning of it. 'Culture' was what the man said down the market, when he tugged at my arm and tried to sell me fake African carvings or a tie-dyed Rasta T-shirt or a full-colour photo of a ripe ackee. In the environment we lived in, 'our culture' had become a sort of mental junk food.

The culture I had actually been part of had no status in this market-place. It wasn't even available any more outside of a collective memory which was rapidly fading as previous generations disappeared. What hit me, though, with an unexpected force and clarity, was that I'd grown up believing, and I still believed, that being a father was like being a link in a chain. My job was to pass on to my son the feelings and emotions which had come down through my own father, the same collective memory which was part of what I was. Suddenly, the memory of my own childhood, its sights and sounds and smells and emotions, had taken on a new reality, as if time had folded in on itself. Suddenly, I had this desperate longing for my son to share those things. Long forgotten and disparate scraps of experience kept on floating to the surface. Chasing rats through the yard, sucking on the sweet pulp of a mango till the juice ran down my chin, watching a flock of vultures climbing into the sky, waking up to the insistent beat of the surf crashing on to the shore. . . .

What made these images so painful was the fact that they belonged to a life which had vanished and which my son could never now enter or even understand. In my own life I had the sense that when I looked back past my father I could see versions of him stretching far into the landscape, at least to slavery. By contrast I had come together with my son on the other side of a break from my old world which had disjointed memory and cut me off from the springs of feeling that flowed from the past. I had the feeling that when he looked past me what he would see would be obscure, a vacuum perhaps, which could be filled only by a constructed 'culture' faked up from the fantasies sketched out by entrepreneurs and politicians. This was it, I realized, as I sat holding him, early Sunday mornings in front of the telly, watching *Mister Men*. There was a hole in my soul, a cultural thing.

I have three sisters and two brothers. For me this was part of the natural order of things, and after I separated from my son's mum I knew I'd always feel a sense of regret and guilt, because we'd never given him the flock of siblings he deserved. Not that he seemed to mind, and he always said he didn't when I asked him about it. On the other hand, when I thought about having another child I thought about him first, how he would feel, and somehow the thought made me defensive on his behalf; I kept asking myself how he would feel. Opportunities came and went. I felt no urgency or any great desire for more children. One is enough, I thought. My mother raised the subject whenever I saw her. She now lived in the USA, so that wasn't often. 'You're not getting any younger,' she'd say.

This wasn't an idea which caused me any great worry. Something else happened round about the time that my big son, as I now call him, had finished taking his A-level exams. For a couple of years I had been having conversations with my partner about babies, followed by discussions about the biological clock. Decisions were called for. I was neutral about the prospect, until, at odd times, I caught myself thinking about what it felt like when my big son was still a baby. Suddenly I would remember bits of the life we'd shared as if it had been the day before. Lying in bed asleep, next to his mum, I'd wake up with a start as he crawled over me to squeeze himself into the middle, between us, his sharp little elbows jabbing a space clear. When he got his first trike, a wooden thing with red plastic wheels, he'd run it across the floor and smash into the wall repeatedly, laughing like a maniac. When I played my Big Youth album on the record player he'd run to the sofa, jump up and begin bouncing excitedly. Suddenly, I missed him, although I saw him practically every day, as if he'd grown up and gone away already. I still loved him with all the passion I had ever felt, but this was different. I wanted my little baby back.

I told him about it one morning as we drove up the A1, on the way north to see some relatives. He gave me a smile of adult tolerance. 'I wondered about that,' he said. 'I thought maybe you never had any more children because of me. It was an extreme sacrifice, though. I wouldn't have minded.'

I was flabbergasted. I'm not sure why. Maybe because I'd spent so much time worrying about it. 'What about now?' I asked him. He thought for a bit. 'It's okay,' he said. 'Be good to have a little brother.'

Over the next few days I felt a weird kind of peace, as if all the elements of my life were at last beginning to jell. 'Let's do it,' I told her.

During the pregnancy he came to live with us. At night I'd go round locking the windows and look in on him as he lay in bed reading, then I'd climb the stairs. Sometimes I felt like the king of the castle, everything I cared about most under one roof. By then we knew he'd be going away to university in a few months. It will all be different this time next year, I kept thinking, and I'd feel a thrill of something like fear.

My little son, the baby, was born at University College Hospital, same as his brother. I was particular about that. While she sweated through the labour, my big son and I were together all night, sometimes sitting next to her, sometimes standing in the corridor, sometimes pacing down Tottenham Court Road. We talked about football, about what it would be like at university, about my father and what it had been like when I left school. The night wore on and I felt more and more pleased and grateful for his presence. I needed him then, the first time I'd needed him in that way, and he was great, useful and reassuring, like one of my brothers would have been.

When the baby arrived, the first thing I noticed was that he was bruised and battered, a little fighter at the end of a long struggle. Then he opened his eyes and looked at me. How strong a resemblance to his brother, both reassuring and confusing at the same time. Holding the little one I kept thinking about how I'd held the big one all those years ago. Now he was taller than me, he could run faster and beat me at arm-wrestling into the bargain. In my mind there was a circle of forces continually pulling in different directions.

But a lot had changed. In the past nineteen years I had learned to be a father. The pangs and pains and agonies of uncertainty I had felt the first time round had simply vanished. Most of this was about familiarity with what would happen. I knew all about mixed feeding and burping, no problem. I could bring up a kid. I knew that now. The other thing I was about to learn was more complicated. Being a father never ends. When the baby was a few months old I drove my big son up to the university for his first day. Registration, carrying his luggage to his room, looking around. Driving away, his mum cried. Everything and nothing had changed. He wasn't a baby any more, except in some private space of our memory.

Back home I hugged the little one. Before I had him, when I was thinking about it, I'd had a secret fear that my love would be like a cake to be divided between the two children. No such thing. Whatever it was had doubled, simply multiplied by two. The other odd thing was that I'd imagined that being with the baby would wipe out my feelings of nostalgia and loss. Instead, there they were, faded a little, but still, on occasion, as strong and painful as ever.

Entering his final year at university, my big son told me he was applying for a postgraduate course in Madrid. 'I want to be away for a while,' he said. 'Stand on my own two feet, away from you and my mum. Find myself.' I told him it was a great idea. Later on the baby and I watched him drive away down the road, little brother crowing bye-bye. In another eighteen years I told him, that will be you. Then I caught myself thinking that while it was possible that I might have eighteen years left, it was unlikely that I would be around to watch him go and leave me behind, the world all new in his eyes, fresh youth on the brink of adventure. That's the one drawback about the baby. Twenty years ago, when I started this journey, the horizon had no limits. Now I know what I only suspected back then. One day I'll die. With any luck I'll have another twenty years, maybe it will be tomorrow. All that I'll leave is a memory. They'll bring it out and dust it off sometimes. They'll tell their kids about me, and they'll say, That was my father. That's more than a hope. I know that's how it will be. Being a father never ends.

— 12 —

The State of London

London is a city that contemporary film-makers can't seem to get right; over the past thirty years there's been a long list of directors who have used London as a location and managed to render it unrecognizable or grotesque. Antonioni shot a big chunk of *Blow Up* in a street where I lived for a while, but the outcome had so little to do with the London I knew that it might just as well have been made in Prague. In *Absolute Beginners* Julian Temple sets out to capture the same period with frankly embarrassing results. A few days ago I found myself watching *The Crying Game* with a growing sense of incredulity at the fact that the director seemed to be going out of his way to furnish his London background with the wrong accents, the wrong clothes and the wrong atmosphere. In recent times only Mike Leigh has come close to re-creating a recognizable portrait of the city, but his best work is a miniature which doesn't depict much more than a specific period in the history of lower-middle-class life in North London. And that's how it goes. England has no movie equivalent to Fellini's Rome, Altman's LA, or Allen's New York; and London is a city whose repeated exposure renders it invisible, like a series of dots which somehow refuse to coalesce into a whole picture.

I suspect that part of the reason why images of London present such a problem is to do with the resentment and hostility which forms a consistent undercurrent to British attitudes about the city. This shows up in odd ways; for instance, the use of the word *London* as a term of abuse – 'trendy London', 'London cliques'. In comparison, terms like the Great Wen and the Big Smoke are affectionate, but they indicate the sense in which London is a metaphor which encapsulates the kind of modernity that the English have tradition-ally viewed with fear and distaste. The politics of the capital have been plagued by a hostile interaction with central government, which compounded the material problems migrants faced, as well as frustrating and delaying black entry into the political process.

From 1964 on, London was run by the Greater London Council (GLC), which took over from the old London County Council (LCC). The GLC had an expanded catchment area which covered the outer London boroughs, but, in comparison with the LCC, its powers over local services had been enfeebled. Before 1981 few GLC politicians made much impact even on Londoners. Given that its first decade saw the massive inflow to the city of migrants from the Caribbean and Asia, a migrant presence was largely absent, apart from the chairmanship of Dr David Pitt, later Lord Pitt, in 1974. Pitt symbolized, however, the weakness of the migrants in electoral politics throughout this era. A doctor who had studied before the war in Edinburgh, and whose career spanned the entire period of post-war immigration, Pitt had established his surgery in North London during the early 1950s and then was selected to fight Hampstead for Labour in 1959. He lost, but was elected to the LCC a couple of years later. In 1970, while Powellism was still a potent force in British elections, he was selected to fight Clapham in South London, and lost again in one of the biggest swings against a can-didate in the country. The message was clear. As chairman of the relatively powerless GLC, Pitt disturbed no one, but the London electorate was not prepared to allow him into the nation's seat of power. In any case, the relationship of the GLC with the ethnic minorities until the end of the decade was ineffectual and tangen-tial. It had failed at the end of the 1960s to produce a strategy for overall planning in the city. It failed over the next twenty years to do more than tinker with London's housing problems, and it had failed to offer Londoners a political vision which could accommodate the changes which were transforming the city. In London, where about one-third of Caribbean and Asian migrants lived, our involvement in the electoral process was no more than a defensive strategy against Powellite politics.

All this changed after the local authority elections in 1981. The Labour Party, cashing in on Mrs Thatcher's pre-Falklands unpopularity, swept into power in all of England's metropolitan councils. London Labour had been led for a year by Andrew MacIntosh, but a few hours after the election results were declared, a meeting of the new members replaced him with an obscure left-winger called Ken Livingstone. In the years following, from 1981 to the abolition of the GLC in 1987, the ethnic minorities were to play a prominent part in the structure of London politics. Part of the reason for this was the fact that the GLC's powers were relatively circumscribed. Unlike the old LCC it left no physical monuments to its beliefs, and the one policy for which it was remembered, 'Fares Fair', in which it set out to hold down fares on London Transport by using local taxation, was scuppered by the courts before it had properly got under way. The GLC had opportunities, however, determined by the shape of the electoral coalition which its new leader called into being to support and defend his policies.

I sat for a couple of years, not long before its abolition, on one of the GLC committees. Its function was to oversee the 'ethnic arts' in London, which seemed to mean disbursing various sums to various kinds of projects loosely concerned with 'the arts'. It was a curious, dislocating experience, partly because I never felt that I had anything to do with the policy or the purpose of the committee. All such matters had been decided long before I came along. The composition of the committee, for instance, was a sort of pick-and-mix sample of every minority in the city, each of them operating from a background of very different requirements and intentions. In any case, understanding contexts or consequences was never the issue. The slogan I heard repeatedly was 'Get the money out of the building,' and I was never present at any discussion about what we were doing, or why, and what effect it would have on the communities we were supposed to be serving.

I still feel the same sense of dislocation, largely because, in the interval since the GLC folded, its activities have been wrapped in the mists of legend, and part of the legend says that the ethnic minorities flourished under the GLC and furnished the city with a new burst of vigour and gaiety. This was the characteristic colour-supplement view which was the front line of the GLC's defence against Thatcher's attacks. In response, the tabloids' treatment of the entire issue consistently fuelled the myth that the 'loony Left' in County Hall were throwing money hand over fist at gays, blacks and nutters. In fact there was only a tiny budget allocated to anti-racist campaigning and grant aid to groups or projects in the ethnic minority communities (in 1984, the GLC's 'anti-racist year', the total budget of the Ethnic Minorities Committee, which was charged with all these tasks, amounted to £2.9 million), and the budget had to be shared out between every minority which could be bothered to make a phone call to County Hall.

But whatever was happening to the city, or to the other ethnic minorities, it's also true that the effect of the GLC on the Afro-Caribbean minority as a whole was largely meaningless, and at its worst, a disaster. Of course, the experience of the other 'minorities' across the board had similar overtones, but for the Caribbeans the intervention of the GLC played a crucial part in shaping the disadvantages the community would suffer in the future. The importance of the arts in this process was also crucial, because the approach defined by the GLC's 'ethnic minority' arts policy was to have a wide-ranging role in the re-invention of 'black culture' as the signature of the Afro-Caribbean community.

So the ethnic arts committee was a good place from which to view what was happening. There'd usually be between a dozen and twenty people present, sitting around a long, beautifully polished table, littered with the lists of projects and application forms. One of the first meetings I attended featured an application for around £10,000 from a 'community project' in North London. It was for 'research', to enable the applicant to create a range of 'multiracial T-shirts'.

On my way to the meeting I half-expected this application to be interrogated exhaustively. Here was part of a small cottage industry, already in existence. I'd been buying such T-shirts for years. If the grant achieved anything, it would simply inflate the business in an already crowded market with no assurance of success or survival.

The reactions around the table to my intervention ranged from polite indifference to outright irritation. It was a small sum, someone else commented, and the point was to get the money out of the building. The grant was approved, and I still think of that experience as a template for the GLC grant aid machine and the effect it had on the Afro-Caribbean community.

The problem was that the movers and shakers within the GLC had very little understanding or sympathy for the ethnic minority communities as they were then organized. Before the emergence in the early 1980s of 'municipal anti-racism', ethnic minorities had struggled with varying degrees of creativity to meet the problems they encountered. For example, the 'suss law', the provision within the Vagrancy Act that allowed police to stop and search on no more than a 'suspicion' of some unspecified misdeed, had been used to harass and criminalize a large swathe of the black community, particularly in South London. Throughout the 1970s the black community had mounted a long-running campaign against 'suss' which was assembled on a piecemeal and *ad hoc* basis, drawing on all the energies within the community. Similarly, in the aftermath of the Deptford fire in January 1981, when a fire started in a house where a party was in full swing, leaving thirteen black teenagers dead, a previously unsuspected capacity for large-scale organization emerged and climaxed in a mass demonstration – the Black People's Day of Action, which had refreshed and invigorated political activism within the black population.

At another level, various groups had begun to organize themselves around their professional interests or around common political ground. From 1981 onwards, municipal anti-racism altered the entire picture. The energies which had been directed towards political and social self-discovery were rechannelled into raising money from the GLC. It was clear that the GLC politicians were sincerely committed to fighting discrimination, but under their particular rubric, Caribbeans, Africans, Asians of various kinds and Old Uncle Tom Cobley all became 'ethnic minorities'. This meant that, no matter who you were, or where you came from, within the culture of the GLC your identity had to be determined by your relationship to white racism.

The GLC wasn't unique in this. Powellism had created race and colour as the central political fact of migrants' existence, and any issue to do with us had become a dialogue between Right and Left. The ethnic minorities were a central issue in the argument, but who they were and what they wanted remained largely unheard. Afro-Caribbeans were worst affected, if only because the shape of the infrastructure which had developed out of our migration and settlement in Britain was unsympathetic or unrecognizable to the white Left. We had no Martin Luther King, no Malcolm X, no national organization; and the rampant individualism of Caribbean attitudes was anathema. For the Afro-Caribbeans the business of material advancement was still paramount. On the surface we were working-class people who didn't behave as working-class people should.

The anti-racist agenda of the white Left, in comparison, shaped itself around opposition to apartheid, around the post-Civil Rights relationship to government programmes in the United States and around the new black nationalism in the Caribbean and Africa. The radicals in County Hall tended to assemble their view of 'blackness' from these elements, so when it came to the Caribbeans the consensus was that we had to be re-educated along these lines, and a brisk trade in black authority figures from the USA and Africa began. Whatever the issue happened to be, County Hall looked abroad for models and policies, a lesson which the Caribbean community wasn't slow to learn.

Throughout much of the 1980s the developments in the structure of black politics and organization began to slow down and freeze, as every new group and most of the old reshaped their agenda towards winning support from the GLC Ethnic Minorities Unit. If black organization had a radical bent it now became completely rhetorical. By the time Thatcher abolished the GLC, the political and social infrastructure which had begun to be erected in the black communities had been destroyed, and black activists had changed course to become clients of white Left ideology. Black radicalism had been re-created as style, re-inventing itself in the shape of a white fantasy. 'Black culture' had become a branch of a diaspora dominated and controlled by American fashions. Various individuals had acquired techniques for engaging in large-scale corruption based on 'getting the money out of the building', opening the door to a strategy in which the black communities would be ripped off in places such as Hackney and Lambeth under the guise of municipal anti-racism.

After the party ended, the nature of the damage was more or less apparent. During the period of the 1980s when the municipal socialists ruled, a number of figures and enterprises previously unknown within their respective communities had appeared and been hailed as the cutting edge of the 'black arts'. After the GLC they disappeared. Who knows what happened to the grandiose plans for a black arts centre in the Round House at Camden Town? Or the plethora of black 'collectives', 'cooperatives' and 'workshops' which mushroomed throughout that period? Most of them had few or no roots within the black communities, the only reason for their existence being their ability to raise finances from the GLC. Cut off from the stream of funds, they promptly began to die. What they achieved before they left the scene was a recasting of black identity. 'Black culture' ceased to be part of the dynamic process of black immigrant life and, instead, became a commodity owned and directed from outside. A raft of ambitious mobile young people adopted the style of a commercialized diaspora in which the important references were largely American. When the film collectives began making documentaries, their models were American icons and gurus, and most of the artefacts of post-GLC black art could have emerged from anywhere except the British neighbourhoods in which their makers lived. At the other end of the scale black people at the grass roots, both old and young, were further alienated and estranged from the dynamics of their own lives. After the GLC there were no senior black arts administrators anywhere in the system, no spaces which blacks controlled, no avenues by which black artists could challenge the insights of their white contemporaries. The major arts complexes, theatres, concert halls, state enterprises and corporations had no significant black presence, but at the other end of the scale all kinds of organizations and enterprises were channelling their efforts into constructing 'black' orthodoxies. Ironically this atmosphere promoted a marginalization which successfully enfeebled or undermined the developing identities of the ethnic minorities in the city; and for a decade the influence of the municipality helped to trap and isolate their political energies within the boundaries of race and racism. If there had been a multiracial coalition, it had been the sort of coalition a horse has with its rider.

In looking across the Atlantic for lessons in building a multiracial entity, the municipalities had missed crucial pointers, partly because, in Britain, the day-to-day conduct of local politics in the USA was largely invisible to academic commentators and journalists. In fact, urban politics in the post-Civil Rights era were marked by strenuous and consistent attempts by liberal and multiracial coalitions to challenge exclusively white power bases by transforming the political culture in major cities. Hollywood instinctively highlighted the drama of racial conflict or municipal corruption in its narratives about urban politics, but its immediate neighbourhood might have offered a number of instructive parallels for observers in London.

The Rodney King affair, for example, and the riots that followed, focused attention on racial conflict in LA, but they also marked the final collapse of the multiracial coalition which had supported the regime of the former Mayor, Tom Bradley. By the end of Bradley's mayoral reign the blemishes were obvious – financial scandals, his dealings with oil speculators and property developers, the failure to solve the housing crisis or to reconstruct South Central. On the other side, just before Rodney King, LA was a city which had pushed through linkage fees to build low-income housing, and was planning to compel local banks to invest fairly in the inner city. After the Rodney King affair the administration's success in forcing Chief Gates out of office, passing a ballot to restructure the LA Police Department, and appointing a new African-American Chief, Willie Williams, has to be seen in the light of the extraordinary power the LA police represented in city politics up to that time. This was a stage in a major, long-term move away from the traditional, conservative, white control of City Hall, and it was probably the high point of a coalition that Tom Bradley and his supporters had begun stitching together in the early 1960s to challenge WASP domination of city politics, which effectively excluded both ethnic minorities and white liberals.

The persistence of this model in the urban politics of the USA seems to be the inevitable consequence of changing demographics. Its repeated failure throws up a number of preconditions for its success. The implicit philanthropy of liberal ideology proved to be a consistently inadequate motive for keeping separate racial groups together, even if it is able to create an initial alliance. Second, such alliances always foundered in the absence of a common ideological base, even when there were clear common interests involved. Third, such coalitions were established and held together by a history of trust and common effort between elites in different communities, operating as equals. In the recent history of urban politics in the USA, multiracial coalitions could fail even when all these conditions were met. Without them, failure was a foregone conclusion. Widespread disillusion, for instance, followed the promise held out by administrations led by black mayors during the 1980s, but it was clear that their failure to deliver was as much to do with their political environment as with their personal weaknesses.

In London, none of the conditions which might have delivered a workable coalition were present, and after the abolition of the GLC even the hope faded. The rhetoric had made much of the voting strength of the ethnic minorities, but in practice they tended to vote in pointedly smaller proportions than whites. The political culture had changed to a degree, however. A number of individuals from the ethnic minorities had been drawn into the centre of political organization, and at the other end of the scale, the London electorate were now convinced that the ethnic minorities were due some kind of role in the political process. The Labour Party leadership had strenuously discouraged the emergence of a black political agenda within its ranks, but, faced with nominally acceptable candidates, it lacked the political will to resist. A year after abolition, in the election of 1987, three black politicians were voted into Parliament in London seats.

Their success, however, held few implications for the politics of the city. They had no common agenda and no perceptible ideological base within the interests of the ethnic minorities. There were a number of issues which might have furnished the basis of a coherent programme for black politicians. The lives of the ethnic minorities in the city were bounded and determined by discrimination in jobs, housing, education and the system of justice. They had an important stake in such matters as the development of small businesses or the flight of major corporations from the inner city. They were deeply affected by movements in high street banking, by the state of the National Health Service and the implications of urban planning. Anyone could have produced their own list of priorities. The black Parliamentarians pronounced from time to time on these issues, but their judgements tended to be piecemeal and their statements often contradictory, while, as party members representing an electorate and a machine which demanded conformity, they were exiled from the possibility of assembling a common agenda which might have led opinion. In the absence of a consistent direction, the politics of the ethnic minorities throughout the last decade of the twentieth century were preoccupied with miscarriages of justice and police accountability. There were obvious successes, notably the judicial report on police mishandling of the enquiry into the killing of Stephen Lawrence, a young student who was stabbed at a bus-stop in South London. The report condemned the police for their 'institutional racism' and the term was broadened to challenge the practices of a wide variety of other institutions. At the same time this was a process which firmly entrenched minority activism behind the boundaries of race and racial confrontation, and steered around the prospect of their engagement in overall structures of decision and control in the city.

Tony Blair's new government in 1997 brought with it the promise of a new dispensation, and the prospect of the return of a London-wide authority excited speculation about the potential of a new electoral coalition. In the event there was no serious black rival for the post of Mayor, and the electorate voted overwhelmingly for Ken Livingstone, the man who had last offered the vision of a multiracial coalition. The Assembly which supports the Mayor's office featured only two black candidates, one of whom resigned almost immediately to fight the seat left vacant by the death of its MP, black Londoner Bernie Grant.

On the face of it the structure of multiracial politics in London as yet offers no avenue out of an incestuous and internecine obsession with race and ethnicity. But the Greater London Assembly might be an authentic stage in the process of change. Black occupancy of high-profile posts is limited to the Chair of the Assembly and the deputy of the board which runs the Metropolitan Police, but the Assembly has also brought in more than a couple of dozen professionals from the ethnic minorities to serve as decision-makers or advisers under the aegis of the Mayor's office. This may be the tiniest possible indicator of change, but it also fulfils the necessary criteria for progress towards the assembly of a multiracial agenda together with the personnel to pursue it. There is one prediction which can be made with absolute certainty. London's long-term health and prosperity will depend on its ability to re-invent a politics which reflects the identity and interests of its multiracial population. In the meantime, it is equally certain that the vigour and energy of its cultural and ethnic collisions will produce more frustration than opportunity. In this sense the city is tied to the prospects of the ethnic minorities, and the key to its future is the success or failure of its political will.

A Shooting in Peckham

(*Sunday Times*, 6 August 2000)

At about 2 a.m. last Monday morning a car cruised along Peckham High Street, and slowed down opposite the queue of mostly black young people waiting to get into Chicago's nightclub. Suddenly, a gunman sitting in the car opened fire with an automatic rifle, wounding eight people, five women and three men. As the echoes died away, the car sped off. The driver, according to local rumour, was laughing heartily.

The event was one that most British people are accustomed to picturing in LA or New York or Washington, but not in safe old London. Violent crime in the capital has traditionally been more or less confined to predictable patterns, and located in clearly defined areas. It used to be a good guess that a small number of individuals, organized into gangs, were responsible for most gun-related crime, and the motives would be equally predictable – wars over territory and profits, stemming from drugs, prostitution or the protection racket. So, after the Peckham shooting, most commentators stuck to tradition and speculated about drug wars and the import of Jamaican Yardies.

This was the easy option, because, although the Met has begun to discourage the use of the term, 'Yardie-related' is a convenient label for London's recent spate of 'black-on-black' shootings. It locates these crimes in familiar gangland territory, and that idea lets everyone, except for the Met, off the hook. The truth, however, is much more frightening. The present wave of violence is different. This time it's personal. The Met, in a belated recognition of the seriousness of the situation, last week announced a change in the direction of Operation Trident, the specialist squad targeting gun crime in the capital. The personnel of Trident, numbering 160 officers, would now be focusing their efforts on 'black-on-black' violence. On the other hand, no one really believes that Trident's methods can solve the problem. Britain's police force has traditionally employed a mixture of infiltration and intelligence to contain gangs and organized crime. Early in the decade, when Jamaican Yardies began setting up networks in the UK, the Met was momentarily at a loss, then it beefed up its intelligence by hiring and importing gang members direct from the Jamaican source. The strategy backfired when some of the informants went AWOL and started to commit freelance crimes on their own account. But in recent years, the Met, working with a network of paid informers and the Jamaican authorities, has now acquired a much improved picture of what the 'Yardies' are about. Discussing the Peckham incident with reporters, the Met spokesmen were remarkably cautious about putting the blame on organized crime or drug wars. The fact is that the violence associated with the Yardie turf wars nearly always took place within a more or less disciplined framework and followed a certain logic. In contrast, the violence sweeping South London looks like a species of anarchy, against which the Met, and its Home Office bosses, has no credible strategy, and is unlikely to invent one in the near future.

The killing fields extend to Dalston in Hackney, and Harlesden, but the axis of this chain of events is a belt of South London, running from the Elephant and Castle, through Camberwell and Brixton down to Peckham. Leaving aside the presence of a substantial population of Afro-Caribbean descent, these areas have a number of important features in common. They are all relatively poor inner-city districts in various stages of gentrification, where young professional whites have recently begun to take up residence, or visit frequently for the clubs and nightlife.

In contrast, young black people, especially young black men, tend to be trapped in these areas by a disproportionately high level of unemployment, while traditional community structures have broken down or vanished. For large numbers of these young men, growing up is marked by a pattern of school exclusion, routine hostile encounters with the police and periods of detention. The result is an evolving culture isolated from conventional social constraints. Its roots are complex. The highest proportion of boys excluded from school are black, and even if they last the course their careers are marked by induction into a culture of defiant failure.

'Take a look at the graduating classes in our university or any other inner-city college,' a lecturer at South Bank University says. 'There'll be several young black women getting their degrees, some of them mature students or single mothers. There'll be a few African young men. Hardly ever any boys from Afro-Caribbean backgrounds.'

It's different at the other end of the scale. One argument blames the history of the black community's relations with the police in London. At the same time the courts have played their part by treating blacks with a disproportionate severity, handing out custodial sentences for minor and first offences. Several of the young men who come out of the other end are literally unemployable, and the only measure of worth they know is how dangerous you are, the only sanction is the threat of violence.

In the heart of Brixton's commercial centre, a black business-man who was stabbed recently when he asked a youth to leave his shop ticked off on his fingers the number of incidents which had taken place during the previous week less than a hundred yards from his shop.

'Two stabbings, resulting in one death in front of St Matthews, an unidentified white man beaten to death in Coldharbour Lane, half a dozen robberies at gunpoint. That's only what I know about.' He dismissed the threat of organized gangsters with a shrug. 'Those people fight among themselves. But these youths are different. A little while ago two guys came into a shop nearby and saw a man wearing a Rolex. Right in front of the shopkeeper and anyone else in the shop they attacked him, pushed a knife in his face and took the watch. Imagine a professional criminal doing that in an area riddled with cameras and in front of witnesses. They just don't care. That's the bottom line.'

Ironically, the material improvements along the South London spine have merely, for the moment, intensified the problems. Gentrification has been bringing new money into the region, enlarging the market for hard and soft drugs, and bringing in desperate young hopefuls to challenge the estab-lished dealers. Equally the proliferation of clubs and clubbers provides a framework for the practice of the violence which decorates the culture. In a sense the guns are merely a con-venient expression of an established predisposition. Around London you can lay your hands on an automatic for less than a hundred pounds. They come in from Eastern Europe and Russia by a number of routes. Guns can be rented for special occasions, with the proviso that if you use them you have to dispose of them yourself. It's now commonplace in the capital for young people to be searched for weapons before entering a club, and in some areas you can't get into a birthday party without going through the same process. In this atmosphere possessing a gun commands respect, and signals your impor-tance, while the chain of events that lead to a shooting can start from an unwary glance.

'Guys get dressed up in their Armani suits,' says a friend living in a block of flats off Coldharbour Lane, 'and make appointments to settle their differences in the middle of their favourite club, then they take out a gun and start spraying bullets.'

This is a culture whose members make their own rules. Until relatively recently, the black (Afro-Caribbean) community regularly threw up a number of radical activists whose organizations occupied the energies and fuelled the imaginations of the most vigorous young people in the district. Nowadays, however, most political activists are engaged in electoral politics and operate within the mainstream parties, and traditional black radicalism in the area has disappeared or run out of steam.

'There's no Black Panthers UK,' a long-term resident said. 'The Nation of Islam has lost credibility, Race Today is long gone. At the last meeting of the police advisory committee, the only people there were Rastas and young white militants. The hard core of solid black people aren't involved any more. The police say they're talking to the community, but all they see is councillors and council employees.'

'What they have instead,' a black barrister who defends a series of violent young men said, 'is culture heroes who think nothing of shooting people who diss them. The media treat these people as celebrities, and the kids see that the style, the violence and the attitude are the only things that bring them respect. So what are they supposed to do? If they have parents they see them in the role of pathetic menials and they don't want to be like them. There's only one way to go.'

The government, struggling with an alternative to simply warehousing more young people in more prisons with the risk of merely swelling the ranks of the disaffected, recently launched a Youth Inclusion Programme, to be run by the country's Youth Justice Board. In Haringey they asked the local council to name the fifty worst teenage offenders in two estates, which they've identified as being among the forty-seven most crime-ridden areas in the country. The youths will be targeted by a magic bullet of teachers, policemen and care workers in a bid to cut crime by 60 per cent. The last few years have seen the rise and fall of several initiatives of this kind which smack more of desperation than innovation, like prescribing aspirin for a raging cancer. This weekend the shootings and stabbings which will be taking place in London won't be stopped by putting more policemen on the beat, or jailing more young offenders or by stepping up the war on drugs. If there's a solution, it's one that the entire society has to address across the range of institutions involved with young black people's lives. Anything short of that is too little too late.

A Funeral in Delaware

When I arrived in London at the beginning of 1956 and discovered that my older brother had gone missing, perhaps never to be seen again, the grief I felt was immeasurable, and for almost two decades whenever I thought about him the image in my mind was of the serious, frowning teenager whom I had last seen standing by the side of the ship as it sailed away from me. When I met him again in Manchester, I was full of delight at the thought that we had found him after so many years. Within a short while, though, it struck me that he wasn't the boy I had imagined, and it was as if this was a stranger who had appeared in my brother's place. When he died, in autumn 1998, I was deeply confused and disturbed by the way that these two conflicting images of him kept coming and going in my mind.

There was something about the experience which reminded me that we had all been through sudden and drastic changes which transformed or distorted our lives in a number of ways. We had been lucky to survive them, but it was the luck of survivors, and somehow it seemed as if the price had been the sacrifice of our beloved brother all those years ago. We had never been able, either, to shake off the feeling that the man who returned to us had been a *doppelgänger*, a sort of changeling come to haunt us with memories of sorrow and disaster.

He was being buried in Wilmington, Delaware, where he died. We, his brothers and sisters, together with a gang of relatives, some of whom I had never met, arrived the day before the funeral in a fleet of cars and minibuses. Our two youngest siblings, Rose and my brother Trevor, had made all the arrangements with an efficiency and dispatch which surprised me. Perhaps it was something to do with the fact that they had never known him when he was a boy. The rest of us felt paralysed by our emotions, and grateful for their intervention. The last time we had all met like this was more than twenty years before, when my young brother had been on the verge of student life. Now my nephews and nieces, children at that time, were grown men and women, the eldest already a research scientist and a professor.

My sister had booked an entire floor in a nearby hotel for our accommodation. We had all arrived more or less at the same time, and, checking in, we were swept through by a holiday mood as we kissed and embraced people whom we had known all our lives but hadn't laid eyes on for years. There were a few dozen of us, several of us unknown to each other except through the family grapevine, and we had come from various different points of the compass for this event.

Milling around the lobby of the hotel we were conscious of being an unusual, somewhat exotic gathering. My stepsister had come in from Manhattan, another brother from New Jersey, my nephews had travelled from California, Philadelphia and Cambridge. A few others had turned up from Canada, the Caribbean or Guyana. A few were white or Indian, and the latest addition to the family circle turned out to be my stepsister's adopted daughter, the child of an African and a Cambodian woman, who had languished in Phnom Penh until my sister claimed her. Listening to the variety of accents round me I had the odd feeling that I was at an international conference, and it was curiously dislocating to remember that I was actually related in some way to everyone in the room. From time to time my mother or one of my sisters would introduce me to a stranger who looked vaguely familiar, explaining the tendrils which linked us together.

The strange thing was that we had come together because of my brother. The story of his disappearance had travelled around the circle of relatives for over twenty years, and it had seemed a typical tragedy of the time, which was shared by many of the families we knew. His resurrection converted the story into a narrative which somehow defined us, an outline of what we had suffered and achieved. Nothing, it said, could ever keep us down, so there was a curious sense of celebration underlying our gathering in the hotel. It was reinforced by the fact that we were, in a manner of speaking, on show to each other. About forty years before, the core of the assembly – my mother, my sisters and I – had been isolated and insecure, torn out of our familiar setting and almost crushed by the thundering menace of the city into which we had come. Now it appeared that we had re-created everything we had lost, and were at ease wherever we found ourselves.

The first task was to attend the wake, and I had to begin by explaining it to my son and nieces. In the English cultures we inhabited, funerals were swift and economical affairs. In any case, we had long abandoned any strict adherence to the religious rituals with which we had grown up, partly because we were now linked by marriage and friendship to other families who were Jews, Muslims or Buddhists. One of my sisters was now a Catholic, another was a born-again Baptist, another had belonged, for a time, to the Nation of Islam. The ground on which we met had to be outside the boundaries of religion, and most of us had adopted a cautious secularism which allowed us to attend, in rapid succession, one relative's Jewish wedding or another's animist celebrations.

The wakes of my childhood, on the other hand, had nothing much to do with religion. Someone died, and everyone who knew them would gather the night before they were buried to talk about them and mourn their absence. The wakes I remembered were social occasions, marked by large-scale consumption of alcohol and coffee. At my great-grandmother's wake, for instance, one of the neighbours, who had drunk too much, started shouting and threatening to fight, so my Uncle Aubrey had marched him down the stairs and kicked him out into the street. In the meantime, the children of the house, transported with excitement, had told ghost stories and chased each other in the darkness, until we fell asleep exhausted.

As it happened, the event we were attending wasn't a real wake. It took place at a funeral parlour in the town, and they called it a viewing. I had once been closer to my brother than I had ever been to anyone else, but I hadn't seen him for a matter of years, and in the month before his death we had argued, coldly, on the telephone about politics, about the different directions our lives had taken, about my work, about our children and, strangest of all, about London and how differently we felt about it. He had always hated London, and on the telephone he seemed to be identifying me and my brother Trevor with it, spinning out a series of vicious riffs about the illusions in which we were entrapped. I had once felt the same, but now I cut him short, too angry to reply, and that was the last time we had spoken.

Now, facing him in his coffin, I felt a stirring of that same anger. It wasn't so much to do with the fact that I couldn't speak to him again, although that was part of what I felt. It was more to do with the setting. I hadn't gained much of an impression about the town from passing through it, but the funeral parlour breathed an atmosphere which was familiar from the movies. The hall was full of wreaths and flowers. On a lower floor a buffet was laid out. My brother's African-American wife, whom I was meeting for the first time, was dressed in dramatic and glamorous black, her hair styled in glossy waves. This was small-town, black middle-class USA, the sort of place that the brother who had taught me to make Molotov cocktails back in the 1970s would have regarded with amused contempt. About a dozen of his friends from the town came and went. Some of them were white, colleagues from the university where he had worked. All of them, apparently, had been close friends of his, but it was obvious that none of them had known him for very long. He had been in the town for only a few years, but during that time they had worked with him at the university, gone for holidays together in Florida or Jamaica, and attended parties at his house. In the fulsome American style, they spoke now about loving him, and how important he had been in their lives.

I felt cheated, somehow. I had hoped, by seeing him, to reclaim his memory and narrow the gap between us, but it was as if he had disappeared again, drawing around him the curtains of a life I didn't like or understand. Faced with these strangers I felt like a distant outsider. The details of the evening fed my disturbance. My brother's eldest son had been one of the party which had travelled from England. He had been born and brought up in Yorkshire, and, hearing his accent, my brother's American friends widened their eyes in surprise and gave each other expressionless looks. Behind the coffin a shelf of his favourite books had been arranged. In the centre was the book, *Windrush*, which I had written for my younger brother's TV series. Arguing with the older one about England and the English I had assumed his disapproval, and, seeing the book, I couldn't work out whether this was a gesture on the part of the widow, or whether he had really liked it. My mother, her sister Joyce and Aunt Muriel sat together in the front row, their faces immobile as stone. Were they as confused as I was, I wondered, between recollections of the boy and the man who had returned after twenty years?

After the viewing my sister began collecting passengers for a trip to Philadelphia. Her youngest son Rory was a student at the Wharton School, and by coincidence, he was performing in a student revue on the same night. Philadelphia was close enough, and my sister was determined that a party of relatives should be there to support him.

I gave in reluctantly, but my nephew turned out to be a big surprise. He had been small for his age, a boy with a reserved manner, whose childhood had been plagued by the agonizing pain associated with sickle cell anaemia. On stage he was a confident and charismatic performer. He conducted an a capella group of boys through arrangements of satirical songs, and when they came off stage they were immediately surrounded by screaming girls. After-wards I took him, together with my son and a party of nieces and nephews, to a Chinese restaurant nearby.

Rory's girlfriend, a fellow student, turned out to be an Indian girl from Guyana, and, forty years before this, her uncle had been a class-mate of mine. The young people talked easily among themselves. My niece, who had been born in London, had studied psychiatry and was now a social worker in Harlem. My nephew, Luther, lived in Cambridge. My son was a postgraduate at Leeds University, and my younger sister's two boys, Marcel and Rory, had been born and brought up in Queens. They only met at family gatherings like this, but somehow they had acquired a firm loyalty to each other. There was more to it, also, than the knowledge that they were related by blood. Instead, they had somehow taken on, without being prompted, the idea that they were permanently linked by the history of our migration and the experiences which marked it. Listening to them talking with each other on the way back that night, I found myself marvelling at the fact that they had been equally at ease among the students in Philadelphia. We had been surrounded, I knew, by a group who regarded themselves as some of the brightest and the best in the country, and who were gearing themselves up to inherit the most powerful economy in the world. My young relatives had seemed totally relaxed and unfazed, part of the crowd. This, too, was the distance we had travelled.

Perhaps I wouldn't have found the following day's ceremony quite as strange as I did, had it not been for the memory of Aunt Doreen's funeral the previous month. Aunt Do, one of my mother's two sisters, had died in Tottenham where she lived, and the service had taken place in a church in the High Street. The occasion was attended by the people who lived near her in the block of protected flats close by Broadwater Farm. The minister and congregation had known her since the time she moved to Tottenham, and he made a joke about how she went deaf when someone said something she didn't want to hear. When we went to the graveside the women who had shared her regular pew at the church sang, their shrill old voices rising above the clatter of the hovering earth-mover – *God be with you till we meet again*. It was a plain domestic occasion, hardly any different from the services she attended every Sunday.

In comparison, my brother's funeral felt like a scaled-down state funeral. In front of the church a gang of ushers waved the cars to different parking zones, and, inside, another line of ushers conducted the mourners to their seats, and before the ceremony began one of my sisters was boiling with rage and in a mood to walk out. Her daughter-in-law had been helping my mother to her seat when she was confronted by one of the ushers, who told her that those were seats reserved for the family. 'I am family,' she replied. Nonplussed for a moment by getting this answer from an indisputably white woman, the usher eyed her – 'Close family,' she said.

'Fucking America,' my sister muttered when she heard, but the incident was like a symptom of some of the undercurrents I could feel. Paradoxically, I could recognize the elements of the service in my brother's tastes. A small choir sang a selection of spirituals as we sat down, and they were followed by a guitarist who played Bach and the music of my brother's favourite Spanish composer, De Falla. But the moment was deceptive. After the start of the service a line-up of the people whom I had met at the funeral parlour got up to deliver eulogies. The minister, who turned out to be young, white and female, told a story about my brother. It appeared that he had been a regular church-goer, and they had shared several serious conversations about spiritual and social matters. He had often helped to entertain the children of the congregation, who had loved him, and the previous Easter he had taken part in a pageant in which he played the part of Jesus. His empathy with Christ's suffering, the minister said, made him so convincing that he had moved all his young friends and several of the audience to tears. My jaw literally dropped open with amazement. As far as I knew, until he died, my brother had been a passionate believer in a complex blend of Marxism, pan-Africanism and various kinds of black nationalism. At the end of the 1960s the first notable public demonstration he had organized had been when he marched his band of Black Power followers into Manchester Cathedral one Sunday, ordered the Dean out of the pulpit and delivered an oration about converting church property in the city for the use of poor black people. In the time we were together I had often heard him launch into bitterly humorous diatribes about white Christians like this American minister. During his last years in Britain his closest friend among British politicians had been Arthur Scargill. He had worked in the Yorkshire mines and often expressed his contempt for people who came into politics with soft hands. In our last conversation he had exploded in rage when I used the term 'black British'.

Now I had to believe that the mild-mannered, soft-headed African-American gent these people were describing was the same man. Worse was to come. Leaving the church, a man dressed in a robe and holding up a gold-plated cross mounted on a pole walked in front of the procession. I had never seen this before, and at that moment it struck me as embarrassingly pretentious. Bearing the coffin with my nephew Luther and my brother Trevor, it also struck me that the three of us had done this only a month before in Tottenham, and I felt the urge to laugh. 'Can you imagine back in the old days,' I muttered to Trevor, unable to keep it to myself, 'our brother talking to that minister except for one reason?' He smiled, distracted for a moment. 'Not even that,' he said.

In the cemetery the grave was covered by a sort of pavilion lined with seats for the mourners. We placed the coffin on a mechanical arrangement, where it perched while another choir sang spirituals and hymns in professional harmony. A master of ceremonies called us forward to file past the grave in a hierarchical priority – his wife, mother, son, brothers and sisters, remaining relatives, close friends, work colleagues and so on. As we approached, the ushers gave us each a flower to place on the coffin. At anyone else's funeral I'd have been laughing my head off at this ceremonial parody, but in retrospect I can still recall the mixture of rage and grief I felt. At the end of it all, when the machine hummed and the coffin began to slide slowly out of sight, my brother Trevor did a strange thing. He grabbed my hand the way he used to when he was a little boy, drew me to the side of the grave and, holding hands, we watched our brother disappear.

Driving back to New York that night, a weird story went around before we split up. After the funeral two of my sisters had gone back with the widow to my brother's house. They lived in some style, it seemed, like all of their friends, each house separated from its neighbours by a little park. My brother had been a keen gardener, and employed two Mexicans who helped cultivate his roses and with whom he would spend hours conversing in Spanish and swapping stories about revolutionary times. When the funeral guests arrived back it appeared that the gardeners had visited the place and, during the hours of the funeral, cropped every plant in the garden to the roots before they left. Seen like this it presented an air of angry desolation. Even worse, my brother's wife had lost or forgotten her keys and the house was locked and ringed with alarms. Eventually, someone broke a window and got in, but it had been an unpleasant return, full of foreboding.

No one would say it, but it was like evidence that he hadn't finished with us yet. Whenever we met or talked about ourselves he would, one way or the other, be a ghost at our feasts. Even in death he had remained an enigma. In hindsight it wasn't entirely surprising that the people who knew him told a story I found hard to recognize. One of the things he believed was that he could control important aspects of his environment by the exercise of his will. After his first heart attack, my sisters asked me to persuade him to take the drugs that the doctors gave him. He was living alone in New Jersey then, and when I asked him about it, he said he intended to regulate his condition by will-power. If he had to take drugs to stay alive, he told me, he would prefer to die. In the end he had decided to lead a quiet existence, so he had cut himself off from the unstable structure of the family's life and shrouded himself in the suburban verities which he thought would deliver it.

We knew more about him than most, of course. We knew now that he had left London to join the British Army, that he had become an engineer and worked on motorways, gas pipelines and the coalfields. We also knew that he had been a political activist of various kinds, that he had studied in Eastern Europe and spoke various languages, but none of this had ever been translated into a consistent direction in which he could exploit the best of his talents. In England, his life had been troubled, and when he left after twenty-five years he swore never to return. In Guyana, threatened with assassination, he fled to New York, and when I talked to him later about it, he said he wished he stayed, even if they had killed him.

Everything about his life seemed like that: incomplete, agonized, torn apart by circumstances which fuelled his frustration and anger. But if he was a puzzle to us we knew one thing for certain. Whatever he was had been shaped by those first years in London, which had also shaped us. It must have been the reason why, in our love for him, there was a strand of fear. He was, in our imagination, the side of ourselves with which we had come to terms or repressed. More than once, I had seen a glimmer of desperate and murderous fury in my brother's eyes, like the reflection of a red volcano inside. I had seen this also in my sisters and young brother; and in the days after we buried him, one of the secrets which joined us was the knowledge that somewhere in the centre of our hearts we were hiding a precise reflection of his rage.

— 14 —

European Tribesman

On my first visit to Prague, I'd only been there for a few days and I was still full of curiosity and a kind of amazement at being in a city which was so different from anything I'd ever experienced before. It was a bright, sparkly morning and when I walked into Wenceslas Square I could see the statue of Vaclav in the distance ahead of me, lit by the sunshine, his sword uplifted, pointing to the sky. It gave me the peculiar sense of being in some kind of virtual reality, as if I'd stepped through the frame of a picture on the wall and found myself a part of the scene.

This impression was reinforced by the everyday bustle going on around me. Wenceslas Square isn't a square. It's more like a broad avenue through the centre of the city, with a pedestrian precinct running down the middle, pavement cafés, a line of booths selling newspapers, fast food, cigarettes and sweets. Like all the public squares in any major city, this was where most of the country's events had their climax. Every celebration or demonstration that the Czechs cared about had happened in this space. Nearly thirty years ago a student had burnt himself to death under the statue, in protest against the Soviet invasion, and people were still laying flowers on the spot. Walking through the square it was hard to resist the feeling that if the city had a heart, it was beating here.

On the other hand, on this particular morning I wasn't thinking about the past, or about the city. What I was thinking about was the fact that I hadn't seen another black person since I'd left Heathrow. In these circumstances you get a sense of isolation. You wonder a little about what would happen if you were attacked by a mob of racists, or even by a solitary nutter. Sometimes you feel you are the centre of attention – everyone in the street must know you're there. Sometimes you feel completely anonymous – no one knows who you are.

What was certain was the fact that, unlike Western Europe, the countries of Eastern Europe had practically no contact with Africa or Asia. Apart from a few odd students, I thought, I must be the only black person for miles around.

It was at this point that I looked around at one of the pavement booths and saw a young black man grinning at me. He had a light brown skin and I guessed he must be mixed-race. Without thinking I called out to him in English – 'Hi, man.' He grinned even more widely, spread his arms out and shrugged his shoulders. Beside him a white man looked over, said something, and they both laughed. I crossed the pavement and approached him. 'You speak English?' He grinned again. 'Chessky', he said. 'Chessky.'

Now he said it I could see it. He really didn't look American or British or African or Caribbean. He looked like a Czech with a brown skin, rather lighter, in fact, than some of the gypsies I'd encountered in the city. He pointed to me, and I said, 'Anglisky.' Did I look English, I wondered? Then it struck me that it didn't matter.

We talked in halting German. He had been born in Prague. He believed his father was African, but he didn't know him. He ran the booth with his family. The white man beside him was his brother.

Coming away from our conversation I wondered what he would have made of some of the arguments about blackness which were part of my routine experience in Britain. We had met and parted as smiling strangers. We were both 'black', but that merely served to emphasize the fact that our identities were actually determined by language and geography. So much for the mystical ties of colour, I thought at the time, but months later I still remember the pleasure of meeting him, and his beaming smile, and the way that he made me feel at ease, as if I'd suddenly discovered home in that alien city.

I already felt close to home in Prague, just as I had in other Eastern and Central European cities. Not because of the architecture and the decor, of course. It was something more subtle and difficult to pin down. The truth was that there was something about the atmosphere which reminded me irresistibly of London in the 1950s. It had the same sense of reflecting something old yet incomplete, the same sense of drabness and nostalgia, the same indifference to my presence. English friends who know these places tend to come up with the same question over and over again. 'How do they treat you? What about racism?' The answer is that for anyone who lived in England during the 1950s and 1960s, there is nothing remarkable about most forms of racist abuse or harassment. Short of physical attack, any form of racism I encountered in the region seemed more or less routine.

On the other hand, for a person of African descent, travelling in the eastern half of the European continent can be a peculiar and dis-locating experience. At the level of the emotions it's easy to understand why. The prospect of a purely social isolation is bad enough, and, hidden in the imagination, the thought of being isolated in an angry mob, alone among a crowd of hostile, alien faces, provokes an atavistic flutter of anxiety. Growing up in Britain I had no direct memory of lynch mobs, but the image is close to the bone. As a schoolboy, during the decade of the 1950s, the London in which I lived seemed a dangerous and violent arena where I was always conscious of hostile, angry vibes directed at me and anyone who looked like me. In my memory there is a clear sense of being under siege, as if my home was a miniature fortress which I reached each night with a feeling of relief. Among our circle of family and friends, every night was threaded through with recitals of a litany of threats and insults, our daily experience of what it meant to live in England. From that perspective we lived within a fortified pale where we felt secure. Looking to the outside world we could see a map embellished with threatening figures. Here be dragons.

On the maps of our imagination the dragons probably guard a line east of Berlin, and, arriving there, you have the continual sense of being the only black person to be seen for miles around, and perhaps in the entire country. A moment of reflection tells you that this can't be true. In any given country, in any part of the world, there must be a group of students or diplomats from at least one or two African countries, but, in Britain and the USA, it's easy to subscribe to the conventional assumption that any contact between black people and the countries of Eastern Europe is strictly limited and specific. This is an impression policed by our invisibility to the gaze of white historians and commentators. It would be next to impossible to find a reference to anyone of African descent in any history of Europe, and, ironically, even where a 'black' person is unmissable, the commentaries avoid or skate over any discussion of the fact. For instance, the African origins of famous writers such as Pushkin and Dumas are well known, but, remarkably, their critics have routinely failed to explore the possibility that their complex racial identity might have played a part in their work. It's not as if the clues didn't exist. Reading Pushkin's uncompleted novel, *The Negro of Peter the Great*, it would be hard to resist the conclusion that the author had an intense and personal concern with his own status as a black man among whites.

The memory of less notable characters has almost completely disappeared from the historical record. George Augustus Polgreen Bridgetower, for instance, was born in Biala in East Poland in 1779, the older son of Friedrich Bridgetower, a Barbadian who worked as a page to Haydn's patron Prince Nicolaus Esterhazy. Taught by Haydn, Bridgetower made his debut in Paris at the age of nine, followed a few months later by a performance at Windsor. Later he shared the same master, Haydn, with Beethoven, and the two young musicians were friends until they quarrelled over a woman. At this point Beethoven crossed out his jocular dedication to Bridgetower on a sonata (Opus 47) – 'Mulatto sonata composed for the mulatto Brishdauer, the great mulatto idiot and composer' – and replaced it with a dedication to the violin professor Rodolphe Kreutzer.

The tracks of such men, as famous in their time in Moscow and Prague as they were in Paris or Rome, criss-cross the European continent. The African-American actor Ira Aldridge, for example, was a great favourite in Russia and the Baltic States and was finally buried in the Polish town of Łódź when he died in 1867.

These famous artists were the distinguished tip of an iceberg. The obscure and untalented left no memories behind them. No one knows, for instance, what became of Bridgetower's younger brother, and no one, I am tempted to add, cares. The invisibility of black people in this context isn't surprising because the traditional defence of racist and xenophobic attitudes towards us has been the argument that our presence in European society is so recent as to be shocking.

Part of what happened is a feature of contemporary race thinking. White Europeans have long since claimed for themselves the Enlightenment virtues of curiosity and enquiry. According to this view, black people had, in comparison, always been made to travel through one form or other of coercion. The consensus of opinion in the West, however, that Central and Eastern Europe are intractably racist sites, where black people must unquestionably encounter hostility and menace, is usually grounded in a different network of observations.

On the night we started bombing the Serbs, I was eating potato dumplings in a restaurant in Prague and arguing with a Czech professor about Milosevic. We'd actually started discussing the eastward enlargement of the EU, before it all turned into a vodka-fuelled wrangle, but by the end of the meal I was beginning to be convinced that I was facing new territory: different, but more strongly rooted and intense than anything I had experienced in Britain.

When I talked about ethnic cleansing in Kosovo, for instance, the professor riposted by telling me about his origins in fifteenth-century Bohemia, his point being that the rights of citizenship in the East could not be understood outside the framework of its historical and ethnic associations. For a black citizen of a European country, this was like a red rag to a bull, but it was equally true that my claim to Britishness was practically incomprehensible to many of the people whom I met in Central Europe. Giving a talk in Ceske Budejovice, I told the story of two mixed-race Europeans, the plot of my latest novel. Afterwards a woman said, 'I still don't understand about these two brothers. Their father was African, but you called them German and English.' The problem was simple. She didn't understand the notion of a national identity which overrode ethnicity.

One day in the autumn of 2000 I drove into Krakow for the first time at about three in the afternoon. I had come from Berlin, stayed the night with a friend in Szczecin and then spent the previous afternoon in Gdansk, before driving the length of the country down to Krakow. In Gdansk I had toured the old town and driven up and down the shipyards, overwhelmed by their size and brutality; then I had been stopped and questioned by the police, alerted by the sight of a black man driving a car with German number plates. I got out of Gdansk then and drove for a night-and-a-half, arriving in Krakow the following day. I had stopped for a look around in Torun, breakfasted in Łódź, and finally wound up waiting for my friend in a petrol station on the way into Krakow. When he arrived I recognized him immediately, although we had so far only spoken on the telephone or corresponded by e-mail. He looked like a typical Guyanese, one who might have been a young brother or nephew of mine, and no one would have given him a second look in London. He was, however, famous in Poland. He had arrived as a student in 1985, and graduated from the Jagellonian University in 1989 in the year of the first Solidarity government. Subsequently he had become a well-known broadcaster and had been awarded Polish citizenship. I had driven down to see him out of curiosity and because I had two days to kill before giving a lecture at a conference in Berlin.

Later on, at his apartment, we ate a curry which he ordered in from a nearby restaurant, and we talked about Poland and his life there. There were hundreds of black people that he knew of, he said, and if you counted mixed-race children, you could double or treble the numbers. Most of the black people were African, but all the Caribbeans and Guyanese he knew were flourishing professionals, and he still kept in touch with all the young men who had arrived in the same group. One of them was a doctor in the countryside, another a lecturer in Łódź, and another had a restaurant in Szczecin, where I had just come from. The name stirred a memory. Two days before I had seen two mixed-race boys standing on a street corner in a crowd of young people and I had waved at them. The boys had all waved back, but the flow of traffic had swept me away before I could stop.

Together with the old gang from Guyana, Brian said, he ski'd during the winter in the Alps. In the summer they went to Italy or the Black Sea for the seafood. Sometimes they travelled to his Polish wife's village near the Ukrainian border. Their son loved it in the country, and the in-laws were mad about him.

In the evening we went to a community centre in the Nowa Huta to see an exhibition of paintings done by a schoolboy from Sarajevo, who after the massacre of his family had ended up in Krakow. It was a cheerful, rowdy occasion, full of refugees from the Balkans, and Brian turned out to be a huge local celebrity. Conversing in the hallway, we were soon surrounded by schoolkids asking for his autograph or permission to take a photograph with him. It was the same the following morning. Walking around the university and the town square, we were continually accosted by Poles who knew Brian or who wanted his autograph or his picture. On the way back he talked about arriving with his fellow students at the airport in Warsaw. No one had come to pick them up and none of the party spoke the language. Standing in the arrival hall they had been surrounded by people staring curiously, and from time to time a brave child, egged on by his comrades, would dash out of the crowd to touch their hands, as if to check that they were real.

Back in his flat that night he outlined his plans to set up a fund for mixed-race children in Central Europe. I asked him about going back to Guyana or the Caribbean. In return he told me about the warning his mother had sent him during the last year. Don't come back, she had written him. There's nothing for you here.

'Poland's given me everything I couldn't have back home,' he said. 'Education, a job I love, fame and good friends. What more do I want?'

Driving away from the town I reflected on the energy and optimism he radiated. His status as a student had probably helped, I guessed, but even so I could feel only admiration for him.

A fortnight later I received an e-mail from him saying that he'd read my book and how much he liked it. On satellite TV he had seen my brother talking about the politics of the city. 'You boys in London are showing the way,' he wrote at the end.

I knew what he was trying to say. History again. During my

lifetime, black identity had been a complex and developing notion. The double ferment of Civil Rights in the USA and the anticolonial struggle in the rest of the black world produced a psychological account of the relationship between blacks and whites which hinged on the belief that we had internalized the white view of ourselves, the consequence being that we could only see each other as insignificant and inferior – the eternal Other of the white imagination. For black intellectuals and activists the struggles for self-government, and for equality in white societies, were inseparable from the struggle to invent and control their own identity.

This was a crucial element of the background which dominated black attitudes in the diaspora for most of the latter half of the twentieth century. By the mid-1990s however, black Africans were in possession of their own territory from the top to the bottom of their continent, and the process had exposed as a sham the idea that national independence would confer individual freedom. The longing of the diaspora had conceived and propagated this belief for the better part of two centuries; and, in the diaspora, our slogans and banners were symptoms of a programme in which we could capture and remodel fragments of the white world as bubbles within which it was possible to be the subject of our own invention, rather than the reflected object of a white gaze. To step outside the bubble, wherever we had established it – Harlem, Washington, Detroit or Brixton – was, the argument ran, the same as rejecting oneself. From this point of view our identity could only be guaranteed by a species of black collective, and there would always be something corrupt and perverse about the idea of building an independent or individual identity within a world of whites.

In contrast, our lives in London had always presented a challenge to the simple equation which balanced black self-assertion against white rejection, however universally it was endorsed; and the consequence was that over the space of half a century our condition has begun to create the possibility of being black outside the collectivity of blackness.

There were a number of reasons for this outcome. One element of the reality we lived was the porous quality of the barriers between blacks and whites in the city. London denied us the economic strength and physical space to shut ourselves off. Ironically, inside the inner-city bubbles of territorial and cultural comfort we created we couldn't help including a white population which was more numerous than ourselves. In comparison, white faces are a rarity in an American 'ghetto', while geographical boundaries between the races are strictly drawn and socially policed in a fashion that Britain found to be impossible.

In much the same way, the arguments about identity in the American black diaspora since the time of Marcus Garvey drew their resonance from its history of segregation and the physical separation of cities into racial quadrants, but in London the geography of the city gave us a stark choice between joining up or getting out. We had, in any case, arrived, not as slaves or indentured labourers, but as part of a massive drift from pre-industrial societies towards urban modernity, and we had never had any intention of abandoning our thrust into the movement which was shaping our world. Instead, we had been undermined and almost crushed, then declared the rescue of our identities from within a culture which our imaginations had called into existence, a Third World of the mind, the passport to which was a sort of diasporic style bible – music, language, hairstyles.

So in Britain the spaces we inhabited also became territories of the soul, where it was possible to re-create and possess cultures which would allow us to define and control our reinvented selves, in defiance of white permission. In London this was an imaginary territory we had been obliged to share from the beginning. We had no other choice, because at the moment of our arrival we had already been formed by a magpie history of appropriation from the culture we were about to enter. On the other hand, the unshackled looseness of the space created by this process made it possible to reclaim black identities, independent of blackness.

London, a place whose habit was to make and remake itself with each new generation, was the arena of our transformation, and in its turn became a hybrid of styles and cultures. Within Britain its influence is irresistible, and its heterogeneous population has begun to redefine the nature and content of Britishness. In the present day, the ferment which marks the centre of London makes it possible to imagine identities which are mobile and adaptable, formed by a variety of circumstances in which ethnicity is only one of a list of priorities. Right now, if there's hope for a continent struggling to come to terms with the clash between modernity and tradition, it may rest in London's diversity and adaptability; and if this is a dream, it's also a necessary vision, but London is a city made for dreamers.

— 15 —

Coda

The Hanging Baskets of Wood Green

Seton grew up in Wood Green. Or, to be more precise, this was where he had lived during the crucial years of his adolescence. When he left his parents' house to go off to university it was a kind of escape, and for years afterwards, whenever things were going badly, he used to congratulate himself with the thought that at least he wasn't still stuck in the place where he grew up. In the circumstances, when he eventually bought a house in Wood Green, the move felt like a kind of defeat. It was as if he had tried to make it in the wider world, failed, and been forced to look for refuge in the place where he had his origins.

In a sense this was true. For something like thirty years he had been living, more or less happily, in various different parts of London. Of course, he had avoided spending any time south of the river, and East London was unknown territory. Central London was his magnet, and he thought of Camden Town as a forbidden gateway to the hinterland of North London, a border that he had no desire to cross.

All this changed at the time of his marriage. Seton owned a small flat near Notting Hill, an address which had become increasingly desirable. His new wife owned a similar flat in South London, and she moved in with him while she tried to sell it. The disadvantages were immediately apparent. The flat, which had been cosy and comfortable for one, seemed cramped and crowded with two people living in it, and when Seton's wife began moving in her clothes, her chest of drawers, her Welsh dresser and her bookshelves, it was clear that they would have to find new accommodation. When Seton's wife started her pregnancy, the matter became even more urgent. 'A child needs a garden to run around in,' she would remark wistfully whenever they discussed the sort of place they were looking for.

The indications were clear. They had to move out of Central London in order to find the sort of house they wanted at a price they could afford, and one day, Seton, reluctant, but egged on by his wife's enthusiasm, found himself bidding for a house only two streets away from where his parents had lived.

After the flat their new house seemed surprisingly spacious, full of light and handy, unexpected corners. The garden, too, was a surprise. As a boy Seton had been bored by the whole idea of gardening. Now he came home after work with a feeling of anticipation and went out immediately to pull up the weeds and check the growth of the tiny green shoots which sprouted from the seeds he'd planted. Soon after they moved in he bought several wire baskets and filled them with geraniums. He loved the way the thick, waxy green leaves fell over the side and crawled down the wall, and when he thought of the garden during the day it was the baskets to which his imagination leaped.

Later on it struck him that the pleasure he got from the garden had been a fortunate discovery, because for a while, walking the distance between his house and the tube station was enough to throw him into a mood of restlessness and depression. To begin with, the high street looked different. The rows of shops had vanished to be replaced by a giant shopping mall, but the rest of it was as he remembered, and during the first week he was continually attacked and overwhelmed by a flood of unpleasant memories. Pushing his child's pram along the high street he kept on noting markers in a teenage landscape of disappointment and insecurity. On this spot he had been stopped and questioned by the police, suppressing his anger while passers-by glared their disapproval. Standing at these traffic-lights he had considered tearing up his school report, anticipating his mother's disappointment and his father's anger. A few yards further down the road, on the corner near the tube station, his sister, eleven years old, had been walking home from school when a man had leaned out of his car and spat on her. 'Go back where you came from, you black whore,' he shouted.

These events were more than thirty years in the past, but for Seton it was as if he'd climbed into a time machine and, getting out half an hour later, had found three decades of change had taken place behind his back. This impression was reinforced when he met his neighbours. The family who lived in the house on the right were white people. English. The sort of English people who had lived in the district for several generations. Bert worked as a security guard somewhere in the City. His wife Elly was a dinner lady. Elly's mum was a white-haired presence who lived in a wheelchair and cackled cheerfully at the baby when they went past in the street. Sometimes they paused to exchange comments about the weather, blocking the pavement for a moment, the wheelchair tilting as the granny leaned over to look into the pram. The family on Seton's left were as different as chalk from cheese. The mum was Jean, a sturdy Jamaican woman with a youthful, bouncy manner, and three grown-up sons, the noise of whose electronic rapping and amplified bass thundered through the walls all week, except on Sundays, when the sound would switch to the tremulous cooing of hymns, punctuated by a gabble of argumentative sermonizing on the radio.

To Seton, both of these families seemed intensely familiar, as if he had known them for most of his life. By coincidence, when he had lived all those years ago with his parents, the neighbours had been so similar that they could have been, give or take a few minor differences, the same people. He had been about fifteen years old then. Moving in, the first thing he had noticed, with the unerring instinct of adolescence, was the fact that the white family on the right, the Greens, had a daughter of the same age. On the second day, across the garden fence, he had made her acquaintance. Seton could no longer remember her name. He remembered, though, her mass of curly brown hair and her eager grin. That was all, because, in spite of his best efforts, her mother, Mrs Green, was a dragon who kept a stern and tireless watch over her daughter, and he could hardly begin speaking to her, in the back garden or on the pavement in front of their house, before being interrupted by a shrill bellowing from indoors.

'Leave that woman's daughter alone,' his mum said irritably, after this had happened a few times.

There was no point in talking about it, he knew, but it was clear to him that the presence of a black teenager next door had thrown Mrs Green into a frenzy of apprehension, and that, whatever the cost of her vigilance might be, she was determined to resist any further familiarity. Seton had grown accustomed by now to the terror and passion which his mere existence could provoke from some white people. In the circumstances it was clearly hopeless, and he resigned himself to ignoring Mrs Green and Mrs Green's daughter for the duration. The mother at least, he thought, was a dyed-in-the-wool racist whom no appeal would ever shift, and he would probably never have spoken to either of them again, except for the peculiar thing that happened at his sister's wedding.

This was about a year after they'd moved. His parents insisted that the neighbours had to be invited, because they would have to put up with the noise and the coming and going. They won't come, Seton thought, but on the day they were all there, even Mrs Green and her daughter. The strangest thing about this was that although they had never exchanged more than two words, the Greens smiled at him, moved through the house easily and seemed to be enjoying themselves. Even stranger was the way Mrs Green behaved towards Duncan. Duncan was a distant cousin who had arrived from the Caribbean at about the same time as Seton and his family. A couple of years older, he was famous for his charm and self-confidence. He was already an accomplished musician. He played cricket for the junior team of a county side, and at the time of the wedding he was about to go off to university. Unlike Seton, Duncan never seemed disturbed or inhibited by the hostility or unfriendliness of the white people around him, and everyone who knew him predicted he would be a great success. Women clustered around Duncan like bees around a honey pot, and to Seton's astonishment, Mrs Green was no exception. In the midst of the crowd she stood by Duncan, chatting to him, smiling and touching him. As he left, Duncan, casually and seemingly without reflection, approached Mrs Green and, without hesitation, kissed both mother and daughter on the lips.

Flabbergasted, Seton watched them smiling and blushing and waving Duncan goodbye. On the surface he should have been reassured, but a terrible thought now struck him. Suppose he'd been wrong about Mrs Green, and the truth was that she simply didn't like him? For some reason this was a much more disturbing idea, and he would have preferred to be able to keep on thinking of her as an intractable racist.

Thirty years later Seton could smile when he remembered all this. Now that he was a grown man and a parent himself, his perspective on what had been going on in Mrs Green's mind had changed. 'The daughter was a hot little number,' he told his wife. 'And I was a randy little sod with holes in my trousers and lust leaking from every pore.'

Separated from those times by thirty years, he could see himself from the outside, but even so the memory made him determine to keep his distance from the neighbours. On the other hand, he was soon seduced by their friendliness. In Notting Hill where he'd lived previously, the neighbours were polite enough, but most of them were middle-class office workers who decamped for the country at the weekends and holidays and went out for their meals at night. When they met on the stairs or in the street there was nothing to say. In comparison, his new neighbours brought presents for the baby, warned him when the dustmen changed their schedule, admired his geraniums and sent Christmas cards.

In less than a few months Seton's feelings about the place had completely altered. Now he walked in the high street without thinking about the past, his eyes scouring the shelves of the shops for packets of seeds and other useful things, nothing in his mind apart from his baskets of geraniums.

Going out early one morning for a paper he saw his neighbour, Elly, coming the other way. He was about to smile and make some inane remark about what a bright day it was turning out to be when he noticed that she was crying, her shoulders hunched and a bunch of tissues clutched in front of her face. He stopped and looked at her with automatic concern.

'What's wrong, Elly?'

She wasn't hurt, she told him. She was crying, instead, because of the anger and frustration she felt. She told him the story rapidly. She had been wheeling her mum to the bus she caught every day to the day centre near the Town Hall. As she was about to hoist her on to the platform, a young girl had jostled them more roughly and longer than could be accounted for by accident. 'Do you mind,' Elly said, 'not jostling my mum?' Instead of apologizing, the girl had rounded on her, shouting abuse. As a final touch, as the bus moved off, she had turned and, hawking phlegm up out of her throat, she had spat copiously on Elly.

Even while Seton registered his indignation and sympathy, he knew what she was going to say next.

'Excuse me,' Elly said, a touch of uncertainty in her voice, 'I'm not being funny, but it was a black girl. I don't know why she acted like that. I'm not that way. I've never had no trouble.'

Walking on towards the shops in the spring sunshine Seton thought about the incident. A wheel had come full circle, he didn't know how or why. Back in his garden he pottered around his weeding, wondering whether Elly was watching him and what she was feeling. After a while, when he had finished watering the flowers, he looked at the dripping baskets and came to a decision. He started to unhook one of the baskets from the wall of the shed, then changed his mind again, picked up the secateurs and began snipping the flowers. Feeling a little mean he tied the bunch together and walked through the house. Propping the front door ajar, he walked along the pavement to Elly's house, holding the geraniums in front of him like an offering. . . .

Index

The index covers the Introduction and Chapters 1–4, 6 and 10–14. Other chapters are anecdotal and have therefore not been indexed.